Challenging Racism

ISSUES FOR THE NINETIES

Volume 6

Editor

Craig Donnellan

Independence

Educational Publishers

Cambridge

First published by Independence
PO Box 295
Cambridge CB1 3XP

British Library Cataloguing in Publication Data
Challenging Racism – (Issues for the Nineties Series)
I. Donnellan, Craig II. Series
305.8

ISBN 1 86168 021 X

Printed in Great Britain
City Print Ltd,
Milton Keynes

Typeset by
Claire Boyd

Cover
The illustration on the front cover is by
Katherine Fleming / Folio Collective.

CONTENTS

Introduction

Challenging Racism is the sixth volume in the series: **Issues For The Nineties**. The aim of this series is to offer up-to-date information about important issues in our world.

Challenging Racism looks at racial discrimination and racial violence.

The information comes from a wide variety of sources and includes:
Government reports and statistics
Newspaper reports and features
Magazine articles and surveys
Literature from lobby groups
and charitable organisations.

It is hoped that, as you read about the many aspects of the issues explored in this book, you will critically evaluate the information presented. It is important that you decide whether you are being presented with facts or opinions. Does the writer give a biased or an unbiased report? If an opinion is being expressed, do you agree with the writer?

Challenging Racism offers a useful starting-point for those who need convenient access to information about the many issues involved. However, it is only a starting-point. At the back of the book is a list of organisations which you may want to contact for further information.

*****

Stop racism now

Racism affects us all – no matter what our background, religion or colour. But what can we do to make Britain a better place for us to live together in peace?

What is it?

Racism: the belief that some races are superior, based on the false idea that things like skin colour make some people better than others.

Prejudice: knowing next to nothing about someone but pre-judging them anyway.

Discrimination: being treated less favourably because of racial, national or ethnic origins. It happens because of what someone does, not because of what they think. Discrimination can be unlawful.

Racism is . . .

Having to keep relationships secret
'I can't walk down the street with my boyfriend because our families wouldn't approve of us going out together.'   Lisa, 15

Being ignored . . .
'I'm Jewish so I didn't have to sing the hymns at assembly. I thought that was reasonable until the other girls at school started to ignore me because one said I thought I was something special.'   Hannah, 13

. . . or singled out
'I was in McDonald's and these lads said to my friend, "Why are you going around with a Paki?" and pointed at me. Then they made jokes about there being a smell of curry.'
Parveen, 17

Ignorance at home
'My mum says she doesn't really mind my having black friends, but she would draw the line at me going out with "one of them".'   Karl, 15

Not getting the respect you deserve
'I hate the way people speak to me as though I can't speak English, just because my parents are Chinese.

They own a take-away and you would not believe the abuse they have to endure.'   Anna, 18

The facts

School can be tough for minorities
Seventy-nine per cent of black Caribbean boys and 70 per cent of Asian boys and girls said they'd been picked on at school.

You want action!
Sixty-five per cent of 16 to 24 year-olds in Britain feel there is not enough being done to fight racism.

Bigotry won't work
Young people from ethnic minorities are almost twice as likely to be unemployed as their white counterparts.

Racists on the attack
Sixteen to 25 year-olds were the offenders in 53 per cent of racially motivated incidents against Asians and 36 per cent of those against black Caribbeans.

Fighting ignorance together
Sixty per cent of British people said in a survey they would marry people from another race, or be happy for their son or daughter to do the same.

Racists can be . . .

Shallow because they won't look at another person's character or personality – they will only see as far as skin colour, style of dress or the language spoken.

Quick to judge those who are different to themselves. Racists have such generalised opinions that they believe in stereotypes.

Stubborn as they refuse to listen to other people's opinions because they are certain they have the right viewpoint.

Ignorant because they make judgements about other people without knowing the facts about how they live in the first place.

Dangerous because they spread hatred and violence through their beliefs. They'd rather see divides in our society than hope that everyone could live in peace together.

Racism: It can happen to everyone

In the majority of cases, ethnic minorities are subject to racism by white people, but it does work in many different ways. Black or Asian people can have a grudge against whites; Jews against Arabs; Protestants against Catholics; Greeks against Turks; Scots against English . . . Why does the list seem endless? So before you think of the racial stereotype, get to know the person first. You'll realise how wrong your perceptions can be!

What's their problem?

Racists hold their views for a number of different reasons . . .
Insecurity: racists might not feel very good about themselves, so by bullying others they can forget their problems.
Upbringing: many have racist views because their parents hold the same beliefs.
Bad experiences: perhaps they've been in a situation before that has made them dislike an individual from a certain racial group. They may now hate people from the same background.
Fear of the unknown: racists don't understand the groups they despise and have no interest in learning about other cultures or nationalities.
Arrogance: they believe that if everyone had the same upbringing and opinions as them then the world would be perfect.
Intolerance: racists believe people of other colours or nationalities shouldn't be living here.

© MIZZ
July, 1996

Victims of racism speak out

These teenagers know how frightening, upsetting and frustrating racism can be . . .

'Don't they have any feelings?'

'Things are bad for my whole family at the moment. There's not one of us who hasn't had a problem, mum and dad included. We're not the only Bengali family in our area, but we seem to get most of the abuse from neighbours. They have no respect and put rubbish through our letter box and smash bottles outside the front door. When my sister got married we went to the cars and a gang of lads who hang around the flats started to shout abuse – on her *wedding day*. Don't they have any feelings? We have reported things but we haven't got proof of who is harassing us. I'm determined these people will be punished one day with the help of the authorities.'

Mila, 15, East London

'I thought they were my friends'

'Our families have never had a problem with me and Jason going out together, but we've had a bit of hassle from people we'd been hanging around with.

'We met in a nightclub and when we started seeing each other a few of my "friends" made comments about me being better off going out with a white bloke. Jason's also had people saying they can't understand why he'd want to go out with a white girl, so the problems have come from both sides.

'I started to get abusive phone calls at one point, so I got the police involved. They traced the calls to a girl who I used to think of as a good friend. I couldn't believe it – we'd

been to a school where there were all religions and cultures, and had grown up with people of all races. I could never have thought of her as racist.

'We don't feel at all uncomfortable about our relationship – Jason and I have even gone on *The Basement* on ITV to talk about how we feel. I don't love Jason because of his colour, I love Jason because of the person he is and I just wish ignorant people would understand that.'

Melissa, 17, West London

'Racism makes me determined to do well'

'I wanted to get a Saturday job so I asked around a lot of the shops in my area if they needed anyone. The answer was no, but I knew it would be hard because jobs are difficult to come by. Then a friend said that they needed someone at the chemist where she worked. She got me an interview but the manager was really off with me and he didn't ask me many questions about myself, which I thought was strange. I got a call almost straight away to say the job had gone to someone else, but I know the girl who got it in the end and she didn't have an interview until after I'd got the call. I can't think there was any reason other than the fact I am black – I was better qualified than the other girl, who'd never worked in a shop before. It really hurts when you encounter that sort of thing but it makes me angry and more determined to be a success.'

Carol, 16, Birmingham

'What did we do to deserve this?'

'My mum put an advert in a free ads paper because we had loads of stuff in the attic we wanted to sell. We went out and on return there was a message on the answer phone from a guy ringing about the stuff. He'd obviously realised dad was Indian from his accent on the machine so subjected us to the sort of language and abuse that was so disgusting it made me feel ill. What had we ever done to hurt him?'

Rubina, 15, Manchester

'Doesn't she belong?'

'I took a friend of mine along to a party and she was the only white girl there. One of my friends came up to me and asked why I'd brought her along because she didn't belong with us. I told her I could choose my own friends.'
William, 15, Bristol

'Don't ignore racism'

'I have a Saturday job as a checkout assistant in a supermarket. A couple of weeks ago I went to relieve my supervisor from the till and there was a posh middle-aged white lady waiting to be served next. She had a look of horror when she saw my supervisor getting up to go and realised that I would be the one serving her. She started to shout at the top of her voice, said she didn't want the shopping if she was going to be served by me. At first I was really surprised but then I became angry when I saw that my supervisor was actually going to sign back on instead of standing her ground.

'While the lady was packing her shopping she started to make comments about black people, saying they shouldn't be allowed to work and should all be kicked out of the country.

'I was so angry, I'd never encountered racism like that before. I'm really glad that I didn't argue with her because I wouldn't want to have given her the satisfaction, but I don't think people should ignore racists either – we should take action and report the problem.'

Lisa, 17, Southend

'Can't they see more than my colour?'

'My mum is from The Philippines and my dad's English. But people are not interested in that and show their ignorance by calling me "Chinky" at school, and going on about slanting eyes. I wish everyone was like my mum and dad. They love each other even though they come from totally different backgrounds and cultures.'
Tom, 14, Edinburgh
© MIZZ *July, 1996*

Despair of children in race jibes

Bullies drive them suicidal

Every black or Asian child in Britain has suffered racial abuse, it was claimed yesterday.

Many have been driven to self-mutilation and suicide by taunts and bullying.

And some youngsters hate their colour so much that they try to rub off their skin, says a report by charity ChildLine.

One victim told a ChildLine counsellor: 'I hate myself, I hate my father – he made me black.' Another, a 16 year-old mixed-race boy, said: 'I feel like killing myself sometimes.'

They were just two of the 1,616 children whose plights were used to compile the 53-page report.

'You would be hard put to find one child from an ethnic background who hasn't suffered from racial abuse,' said Mary MacLeod, ChildLine's research director.

'Children find it just as hard to talk about as those suffering sexual assault because they feel shame and despair, which makes it extremely difficult to put their pain and distress into words.' ChildLine offers confidential telephone advice to despairing children. Executive director Valerie Howard called for schools to tackle bullying and allow pupils of different backgrounds to discuss and explain their cultures.

She added: 'Racial abuse can lead to self-mutilation where children try to rub their colour away. It can also lead to a rebellious nature or force children to run away from home.'

The Commission for Racial Equality, *Mizz* Magazine and Crime Concern were also involved in the report's production.

CRE researcher Marc Jaffrey said: 'This is not about political correctness, it's about a significant number of British children suffering abuse and violence. It can lead to failure in school, loss of friendships and withdrawal into self. Suicide is a factor among young people who are subject to racial abuse.'

The report is to be distributed to thousands of teenagers through *Mizz*, and schools and youth clubs are to be given a 10-point action plan on how to combat racism.
© *Daily Express*
July, 1996

Suicide agony of boy tormented by racists

Police study anguished diary that recorded bully attacks

A schoolboy left a poignant epitaph revealing his secret torment at the hands of bullies before hanging himself.

With tragic irony, Vijay Singh's Poems About Bullies was seen by an unsuspecting teacher.

She congratulated him and wrote underneath: 'Excellent work Vijay.'

But she did not know that it was not only based on his cruel experiences, but was also a cry for help. The 13-year-old boy told no one of his agony.

Last night detectives were delving into the background of the hate campaign suffered by Vijay, who told his loving parents he had been taunted because of his turban.

Police were studying a diary and the felt-tip poem left by Vijay who was found hanging by a silk scarf from a banister at his home.

The officer leading the investigation, Det Sgt Phil Wrenn, said he was investigating whether Vijay had suffered abuse at the hands of race-hate pupils to and from school. He told *The Express*: 'I am treating this very seriously.

'Although I am not looking for anybody directly for Vijay's death, I will be conducting a thorough inquiry and may pass my papers to the Crown Prosecution Service for consideration.'

Mr Wrenn described the case as 'very tragic' and one which had hit a close and respectable Sikh family.

Entries into Vijay's heartbreaking diary read: 'I shall remember this for eternity and will never forget.

Monday: My money was taken.
Tuesday: Names called.
Wednesday: My uniform torn.
Thursday: My body pouring with blood.
Friday: It's ended.
Saturday: Freedom.'

By Shekhar Bhatia

His body was found at his home in Stretford, Manchester, in the early hours of Sunday after his family had returned from a party.

Neither his devastated father Jagtar, friends nor school counsellors knew of Vijay's torment, despite the fact that only days before his death he had written a chilling account of bullying for an English lesson.

He received a merit mark at Stretford High School for the graphic poem.

Yesterday Vijay's distraught mother Nickey told of her shock and heartbreak. In tears, she said: 'We're completely shocked. We discovered a diary of bullying in his jotter pad and that is the only clue. His last schoolwork was about bullying. He was a dream son.'

Stretford High School was one of the first in Britain to appoint a full-time school counsellor to deal with any problems children may find either in or outside school. Yesterday teachers said they had no idea how Vijay slipped through the safety net.

But friends revealed that the Manchester United fan had been bullied by pupils from other schools and had been the victim of taunts on the football pitch.

Vijay, the eldest of six children, never saw a match at Old Trafford because his father feared that his turban-wearing son may fall victim to taunts.

Headmistress Barbara Howse refused to comment directly on the bright young pupil's death, but a statement given to other shocked pupils said: 'Vijay was a superb member of Stretford High School and will be greatly missed by all of us.'

Last night it was revealed Vijay had been so concerned about his younger brother also being bullied, he enlisted the help of a schoolfriend to keep watch on him when he went on holiday.

Vijay's funeral, which will be attended by classmates, will be held at Manchester's Southern Cemetery today.

© *Daily Express*
October, 1996

Poems about bullies

I'm frightened and scared
My body has been shaking
My mouth open wide and frozen, the tears drop as they destroy my face
take my money and flee
to where they can go. Bullies
I call out they have no feelings at all.

Bullies are the people who have no feelings or emotions. They are people who are not so clever at things that others are. They do this because they have no skill for anything else and know they need skills for this.

Bullies are Bad and selfish people. They're also cowardly people, cruel and evil people. They are more than all this but they're also guilty. They hurt us with words, hurt us with body contact, but not clever.

Vijay

Racism 'makes young try to rub off colour'

Racism makes some black children so unhappy that they try to rub the colour off their skin, a report said yesterday.

Many children from ethnic minorities have to put up with racial harassment every day, said the study by ChildLine, based on the records of more than 1,600 young callers to the helpline.

Ten-year-old Rita told ChildLine counsellors: 'They call me Paki and shout, "You don't belong in this country".' Another victim said: 'I hate myself. I hate my father because he made me black.'

Callers came from a wide variety of ethnic backgrounds including African, Afro-Caribbean, Asian, Chinese, Jewish, Irish and Spanish. Most saw themselves as British.

The report was launched at a joint news conference held by ChildLine, *Mizz* magazine, Crime Concern and the Commission for Racial Equality.

Herman Ouseley, chairman of the commission, disclosed: 'When I was a young child in 1957, night after night after night there was another bottle coming through the window. I didn't complain. There was no one to talk to.'

Children suffering racism can find it just as hard to talk about it as those suffering abuse or sexual assault

---

One in four ethnic callers said they had been bullied and one in eight had experienced racism within their families over 'forbidden relationships'. Some 216 said they were torn between their own desires and those of their parents.

The four organisations have united to highlight the extent and nature of racism in Britain and to provide support, help and advice in coping with and tackling racism.

Mary MacLeod, the report's author, said: 'The diversity of children ringing ChildLine about this issue shows that racism has the potential to affect all children, not only those designated black or ethnic.

'Children suffering racism can find it just as hard to talk about it as those suffering abuse or sexual assault because they feel shame and despair, which makes it difficult to put their pain and distress into words.'

Marc Jaffrey, a researcher who works for the commission and who helped to compile the report, said: 'This is a serious threat to the growing diversity and tolerance in Britain.'

The report is to be distributed to thousands of teenagers through *Mizz* magazine. Every school and youth club is to be targeted with a 10-point action plan on how to combat racism.   © *The Telegraph Plc London, 1996*

Racism incidents

Incidents reported to the police in England and Wales in 1988, 1994/5 and 1995/6

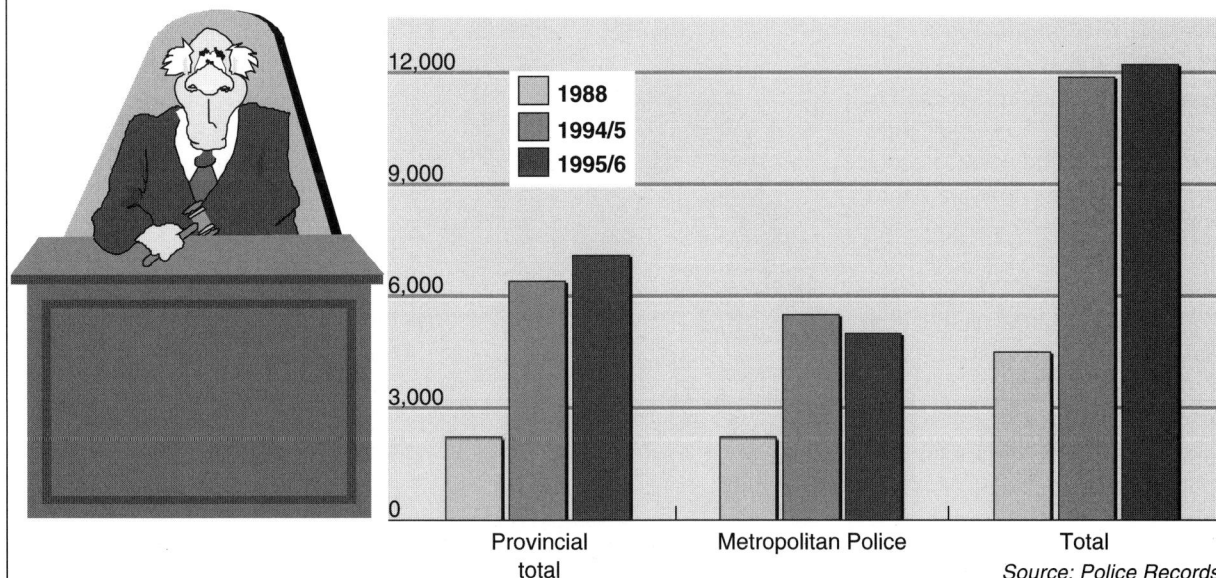

- 1988
- 1994/5
- 1995/6

12,000
9,000
6,000
3,000
0

Provincial total   Metropolitan Police   Total

Source: Police Records

Shades of prejudice

Children of mixed-race families often have to face a double dose of abuse and rejection, notes Chris Dunkerley

They sit huddled together on the sofa. Jacob, from Pakistan, his white Scottish wife Maureen and their three-year-old daughter, Sally. They fear harassment from racist gangs, they fear discrimination from the white and Asian community. Most of all, they fear for their mixed-race daughter.

'Children of mixed marriages have a lot of hassle,' says Jacob.

They are not welcomed by either of the two communities, they are trapped somewhere in the middle.

The Scottish Office does not collect specific statistics on mixed-race families. The 1991 census was the first to ask about racial origin, but there was no box to tick for people of mixed race.

There is a growing movement in the United States calling for an official mixed-race classification, arguing that these people have their own culture and their own identity.

So what about our mixed-race families? Where do they belong?

When the British Government collects statistics, it has boxes for white, black, Asian, Chinese but for mixed race there is only the demeaning 'other'.

Perhaps the assumption is that having a foot on both sides of the fence allows them to choose and be accepted by both black and white. But for many families this is not the case and help is very difficult to find.

Mixed-race families and their children often face a lonely struggle for identity.

Donald Duggan is a minister in Eyemouth on the Berwickshire coast. It's a long way from his upbringing in south-east London as the child of a Jamaican father and white mother. 'Being mixed, you're not accepted by either side,' he says.

He was the only non-white child at primary school. 'If they didn't call you fat, thin or skinny, they'd call you something else.'

Yet he also found rejection from the large black community. 'Black people don't accept you because you're not full-blooded. You're in the middle. I thought of myself as mixed up. Not in one camp or the other. I was British with a black skin. I was angry.'

The McCrum family live in West Lothian. They have been subjected to racist phone calls and their three cars have been badly vandalised. Larry McCrum and his Kenyan wife, Mukami, have a 22-year-old son, Ndegwa, and an 18-year-old daughter, Jambi.

Ndegwa was not keen to talk about his experiences. His mother explains: 'He's reacted to what happened differently.'

'To my mind one of the mistakes he made when he was younger was to model himself on me,' says Larry. 'He wanted to take a white identity because he could see the power structure lay there.'

Nevertheless, the police and neighbours in their last town saw him as black.

If a window was broken, they came looking for Ndegwa and at school he suffered from the inevitable taunts from children who also saw him as black.

'We taught him about peace,' says Mukami, 'but he'd come home from school crying, so I said, "Hit them before they hit you." He did, and he got punished for it.'

Jambi adopted a different approach. She searched for an identity in primary school.

'I asked the teacher not to let me sit in the sun in case I became darker,' she says laughing. 'Later, I went through a phase of wanting to be like mum, with my hair braided. Then like dad, with my hair straight. I even stopped eating, not to become thin but to become pale.'

Jambi's parents eventually sent her to Mary Erskine's School, a fee-paying school in Edinburgh, hoping that after their son's experiences it would give Jambi a more secure environment in which to grow. It proved to be the right choice.

'Mixed-race children often want to be white or black because they want to fit in,' asserts Jambi. 'I decided to make a path for myself. I see myself as brown in colour. My mother is black, but I watched *Braveheart* and I was there with them. I'm Scottish, too.'

Jambi jumps off the sofa and switches on her computer. 'Look. I've written this stuff down. I'll print it out for you.'

It reads: 'You are special. Always remember that you come from a long line of great people. Always be true to yourself.

'I am happy knowing that my experiences have made me a strong person and I know my identity. I am a young Kenyan Scottish woman and nobody can take that away from me.'

All schools have an anti-racism policy, but maybe Mary Erskine's takes it more seriously than most. The first listed aim of the school is, 'To value equally all members of the school community.'

Deputy head Norma Rolls says: 'We follow Christian principles and try to promote mutual tolerance and a friendly atmosphere, in which pupils from all ethnic, cultural and religious backgrounds feel welcome.'

Ruth Johnson lectures in education, specialising in race.

She is part Chinese, part Indian, and married to Mark, who is white Scottish. They have two children

and their biggest concern is not racist taunts, but the school curriculum.

'Our children will learn a lot about Mark's history,' says Ruth, 'but not about who I am. Where different cultures are included it's with a tourist-eye view. If half your background is seen as having no value, it's better to deny it. What's that going to do to you? You'll come home like our son Andrew did and say "Brown and black is dirty".'

'We think we're fair,' continues Mark. 'The Scots have been oppressed too. 'But the differences we are used to are class and nationality. We have less of a history of diversity of race than England. We don't know how to celebrate mixtures.'

Scotland should be a good place for mixed-race families, but the ChildLine report on children and racist bullying, published two weeks ago, scotched that myth.

Its Scottish director, Anne Houston, confirmed that a significant number of the calls they receive are from mixed-race children.

'They speak more clearly than I ever could,' she says. 'Mixed-race children are having a difficult time.'

Jambi McCrum agrees. 'People often ask me which country I feel I belong to,' Jambi says. 'As much as I love Scotland and feel dedicated to it, deep down inside I do not feel that Scotland wants me.' © *The Scotsman August, 1996*

Call to guide children from evil of racism

By Hannah Cleaver

The Commissioner for Racial Equality in Wales last night called for racism to be tackled in schools as part of the national curriculum.

Ray Singh, one of just a handful of ethnic minority barristers in the UK, said the only way to encourage black and Asian people to join the criminal justice system and for the system to treat them fairly was to start from the beginning.

He spoke as new figures were released which appear to show the British justice system is unfair to the ethnic minority population which in turn shuns it, enabling racism to continue virtually unchecked.

Mr Singh, who for a number of years was the only barrister in Wales of minority ethnic origin, said action should be taken in schools to break this circle of disaffection and discrimination.

'It has to start at the very bottom in education, where the teachers should have curriculum training with bullying and racism and educate the children that they are all the same,' he said.

'As an example, Bangladeshi girls are told to do domestic science

at school "because they will be getting married soon" and told there would be no point becoming a doctor or a lawyer. That kind of attitude must go.

'It is at the grass-roots level we have to educate people. Fifteen years ago I said to the ethnic minority people to open our doors to our neighbours. Let them see there's nothing wrong with the way we live. Let our children merge with our neighbours. Some try to keep their children to themselves, fearing they will be bullied. I think children coming together, knowing that racism will not be tolerated in schools from day one, is the way forward.'

Mr Singh, who practises as a barrister at Swansea and sits as a deputy judge in North Wales, said he was saddened by new figures from the National Association of Probation Officers and Association of Black Probation Officers which showed that people from ethnic minorities were over-represented in prisons and under-represented as

professionals within the criminal justice system.

The national association's assistant general secretary, Harry Fletcher, co-author of the report, *Race, Discrimination and the Criminal Justice System*, said there was a definite link.

'The experience generally for the majority of black people is that they see the justice system as something which will impinge negatively on their lives. They are less likely to think of the criminal justice system as a positive career route.'

All the High Court judges are white, with just five circuit judges out of 514 coming from ethnic minorities, two district judges out of 339, 13 recorders out of 897 and nine assistant recorders out of 341.

The picture is similar throughout the stages of the system.

Mr Singh, who belongs to a section of 6 per cent of barristers who are from ethnic minorities, said, 'I have been encouraging the magistrates to recruit ethnic minority people and they are appointing them now as JPs. A number of appointments have taken place in Swansea and farther east, in Port Talbot as well as Cardiff and Newport. If they are involved in the system they can redress the balance.

'I describe myself as from Asian origin. I was the only one in Wales for many years. It is only in the past four or five years that two have come to South Wales and another one or two in North Wales.

'It's difficult for black and ethnic minority members of the bar to find pupillage and chambers.'

The number of people from ethnic minorities on the other side of the criminal justice system is also disproportionate to the number within the general population.

Black and Asian people are five times more likely to be stopped on the street by police than white people. Nearly 17 per cent of all prisoners are from ethnic minorities, an increase in the proportion on 1989.

Of sentenced prisoners, 11.5 per cent are black, again an increase on the last figures.

Jail governors at foot of list

The racism survey published today shows judiciary has just 1.3 per cent people from ethnic minorities, a performance which is better only than that of prison governors who score a tiny 0.49 per cent.

The number of magistrates who are from ethnic minorities is not even known, while magistrates' court staff score 3.9 per cent, Criminal Prosecution Service staff 7.5 per cent and the police 1.75 per cent.

Prison officers are 2.4 per cent ethnic minorities, all other prison staff 2.74 per cent and probation grades 7.6 per cent.

Racially motivated crime has increased by 411 per cent in South Wales and people from ethnic minorities are five times more likely than whites to be stopped and searched by the police.

They are more likely to be on probation and in prison than their white counterparts.

Of British men in prison, 12 per cent are from an ethnic minority compared with 5 per cent of the general population.

Black men make up 9 per cent of prisoners despite being just 1 per cent of the population.

© *Western Mail*
August, 1996

Racial abuse is problem in Scots schools

By Sarah Urquhart

Many children in Britain are the victims of racial abuse and racially motivated violence, according to a report published yesterday.

In Scotland there is also the problem of racism against English children, according to Ms Anne Houston, director in Scotland of the charity ChildLine.

The report, which was launched by ChildLine, the Commission for Racial Equality, *Mizz* magazine, and Crime Concern, cites examples of racism at school, in the home, and on the streets, against people from a wide variety of cultural backgrounds including African, Jewish and Asian.

'Racism is often under the guise of bullying. This happens to a certain extent to children who come from England. The issue of difference seems to be difficult for children,' she said.

In one case, a 13 year-old who came to Scotland five years ago still had no friends because she was English. There were also incidences of abusive name-calling against English children.

An American child who had moved to Scotland complained of being verbally abused, saying: 'I get lots of hassle. My parents tell me to ignore it but I can't. Some nights I cry myself to sleep.'

Ms Houston said that there were also many examples of racism against children of different ethnic groups in Scotland. She said: 'There is a risk that we can think it isn't an issue for us. It is often thought that racism is not a problem in Scotland, but from what children are telling us it is.'

The ChildLine report was written by the charity's research director Ms Mary McLeod and is based on the caller records of 1,616 children. In half the cases, racial bullying had been going on for over one year, and many callers said it was a feature of their entire school life. As well as being victims of verbal abuse, many described being physically assaulted, and having their possessions stolen or destroyed.

One caller, Lara, 13, was set upon by three boys on her way home from school, who shouted abuse at her and poured petrol over her head and shoulders. She was now terrified of walking to school.

Ms McLeod said: 'The diversity of children ringing ChildLine about this issue shows that racism has the potential to affect all children, not only those designated black or ethnic minority.'

She added: 'It is vital that every aspect of our society unites to oppose racism, providing these children with positive imagery of themselves and their communities in order to strengthen their confidence and identity.'

Crime Concern, the national crime prevention agency, has been working to counter racism through its Prudential Youth Action Initiative as well as its other crime reduction programmes.

Ms Houston said as well as raising general awareness it was essential to include young people in solving the problem of racism.

© *The Herald*
July, 1996

Ethnic minority children 'still suffer racism daily'

Callers to charity helpline give insight on lives 'blighted by bullying'

By Stuart Millar

Ethnic minority youngsters are still suffering blatant racial harassment on a daily basis, according to a report published by the charity ChildLine yesterday.

Despite years of progress in race relations the lives of many young people were being blighted by unrelenting bullying and abuse, it said.

Researchers analysed the case records of more than 1,600 callers to the charity's helpline who had experienced racism in the year to March 1995. Although they formed a tiny percentage of the 90,000 callers in the period, ChildLine insisted that the findings were significant.

Callers came from backgrounds including African, Afro-Caribbean, Asian, Jewish and Irish. Most described themselves as British.

In many cases, the perpetrators were other young people. One in four callers said they had suffered racist bullying. Many were afraid to discuss it with their families or teachers.

A girl aged 13 said she had been attacked after school by three boys who poured petrol over her and called her names. She was now terrified of walking to school.

Ethnic minority children in predominantly white schools were most at risk of harassment, the report concludes. Around 75 per cent of those bullied described themselves either as the only one in their class or school or as one of very few similar children.

More than one in eight had experienced racism in the home – usually those who were in relationships their parents found unacceptable. Around half described their families as racist. Some had come to resent their parents. One caller told the counsellor: 'I hate myself, I hate my father. He made me black.'

Valerie Howarth, ChildLine's chief executive, said: 'These are not isolated incidents. For many young people these are a way of life.'

> *A girl aged 13 said she had been attacked after school by three boys who poured petrol over her and called her names. She was now terrified of walking to school*

Herman Ouseley, chairman of the Commission of Racial Equality, which is supporting ChildLine's campaign, along with *Mizz* magazine and Crime Concern, said the findings reminded him of his experiences as a child in the 1950s. 'For too many young people, growing up in Britain today means facing racially motivated violence and persistent racial discrimination.'

'I'm coloured. They call me nigger and black bitch. I just want to be respected.'
Mandy, 14

'I am being bullied by girls at school because I'm slightly tanned. It's been going on for five years. My mum says ignore it, but I can't.' Simone, 12

'I'm half-caste. I've been bullied about it for 10 years. I feel like killing myself sometimes.' Jason, 16

'Mum has left because dad was hitting her. Now he's hitting me and calling me "half-breed" and "nigger" because my mum is black.' Lesley, 12

© *The Guardian*
July, 1996

Ministers in school anti-racist drive

Tory attacks on 'loony left' programmes are reversed

By Donald MacLeod, Education Correspondent

Conservative ministers yesterday reversed more than a decade of attacks on 'loony left' classroom policies and instructed schools to adopt anti-racist and multicultural programmes to help students from ethnic minorities.

The move infuriated Tory backbenchers but was welcomed by teachers as a return to the equal opportunities policies of the Inner London Education Authority (ILEA) abolished by the Thatcher government.

'Colour blind' policies in schools had failed to tackle inequalities, and the performance of African and Caribbean pupils – six times more likely to be expelled than their white peers – was of particular concern, said a report from the Office for Standards in Education (Ofsted) published yesterday.

In the past 10 years there had been dramatic improvements in exam results among some minority groups such as Bangladeshi children in inner London, but the gap between the highest-and-lowest achieving groups was growing. Asian pupils were most likely to be bullied, and there was an 'unusually high degree of conflict between white teachers and African-Caribbean pupils'.

Cheryl Gillan, the Education Minister, said the Government would pursue a range of initiatives in schools in collaboration with the Commission for Racial Equality, including ethnic monitoring and schemes to tackle racial stereotyping. 'Some ethnic minority pupils do extremely well but others achieve less than they could. This is a real cause for concern. The Government takes it very seriously and is determined to tackle it.'

Harry Greenway, a Conservative member of the Commons education committee, said: 'It is right to have a desire to be fair to all, but the way to achieve that fairness is giving everyone equal treatment. By picking on this group or that for special favours you create inequality.'

The National Union of Teachers, however, said the Government was adopting policies which it once decried as loony left. 'It abolished the local authority which most put them into practice – the Inner London Education Authority – without ensuring its practices were carried on throughout the country.'

Neil Fletcher, the leader of ILEA when it was abolished in 1988, said:

GCSEs

Percentage of pupils gaining five or more GCSE higher grade passes. Both sexes in Birmingham.

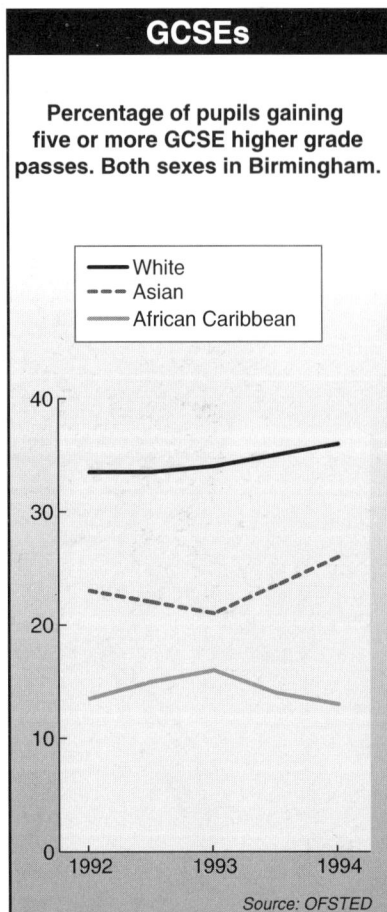

Source: OFSTED

'This sounds like our equal opportunities policy, circa 1983. The difference is that we were putting real money into it.'

Chris Woodhead, HM Chief Inspector of Schools, said schools should do more to monitor by ethnic origin pupils' progress and examination results. He hinted that Ofsted would soon insist on this information during inspection visits.

'Schools must address ethnic diversity, as failure to do so has proved counter-productive. Where schools have adopted colour blind policies, inequalities of opportunity have continued,' Mr Woodhead said. He called for sensitive and self-critical approaches by schools to multiculturalism and anti-racism.

Mr Woodhead has repeatedly told schools they should not use social factors as an excuse for poor performance or low expectations. He denied he was reneging on Ofsted's previous position. 'Schools can and do make a difference. But it would be blinkered in the extreme to pretend that family background, social class or ethnic origin are not also significant.'

Tower Hamlets, the London borough praised by the inspectors for fostering dramatic improvements among poor Bangladeshi children, said its £8 million English language programme was in jeopardy because ministers were dithering over funding.

Peter Miller, president of the Secondary Heads' Association, said he was delighted that Ofsted's blinkers were coming off. 'Mr Woodhead has tried to claim previously that schools pointing to the difficulties they face because of the social mix of their children are just whingeing.'

Children and racism

An extract from Children and Racism by from ChildLine

Violent racist bullying

Children described being punched, hit, kicked, threatened, spat at and beaten by groups of children. One child called about having her hair set on fire on the bus home from school. Some children had been beaten up and had their possessions stolen, others had their things trashed or wrecked – glasses, bags, clothes, books and bikes.

'I'm being bullied by six boys in my class. They call me racist names, chase me, beat me up and take my money.'

Children had been hit by rounders and baseball bats as well as having been kicked, punched and had hair pulled. One girl described her pillow covered in hair following an assault. Another youth talked about having a punctured kidney following a severe group assault, and yet more described injuries requiring stitches and medical treatment. One boy told of having hairspray sprayed in his eyes, others of having been hit by stones. Injuries sustained had included broken teeth, severe cuts, burns, broken noses and limbs, and some children mentioned having been hospitalised, for example an Iranian boy who was burned on the neck with a cigar.

Some of the assaults, in addition to being violent, were thoroughly nasty: one child talked about having her bag urinated in, some others of having their heads put down the toilet.

'I have race problems at school and so does my brother. We're picked on all the time. I get punched and kicked and had my head put down the toilet.'

Nathan, 8, had been bullied for some time by an older boy. 'Today he organised a gang. They came up to me and said "You Paki bastard, give us your money or we'll beat you up".' Nathan had a black eye, torn lip and a bloody nose. Apparently his parents had been to the school without effect.

'I'm Indian. People at school keep calling me names . . . "wog", "paki", "brownie", "chocolate drop" . . . things like that . . . there's been physical violence too . . . they pull my hair a lot . . . it's long . . . they spit and burn fags on me . . . my sister gets it too. I feel so angry and depressed. Mum is ill so we don't want to worry her.'

Sandy, 13, phoned to talk about being bullied; but only later in the call could she say it was because she was 'half-Arabic'. She said she had a 'coloured' friend at the school who was also bullied. 'I don't want to leave school . . . I want to take my GCSEs . . . I want to stand up to the bullies.' Sandy was bright and had been moved up a year at school. She had been threatened with a knife a number of times, and pelted with bananas on the way home from school. She had told the school about the bullying, but not the 'serious' part of being threatened; she had been advised to face the bullies and stand up to them.

'They call me "Paki" and "chocolate chip" and they won't let me go to the toilet . . . they say it's for white people only.'

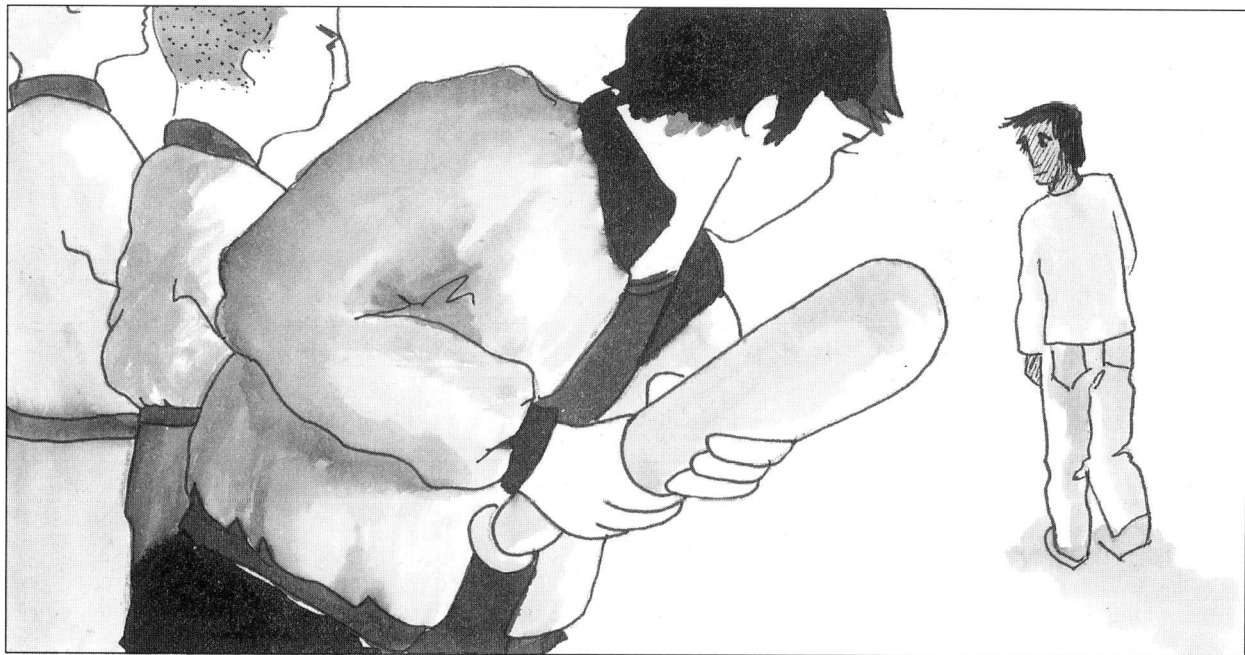

Corra, 14, was Irish. She and a black friend were being bullied by a group of six girls. The bullying was racist, they call her IRA and other names. She had been pushed off her bike and broken her arm and leg. Though her parents had gone to the school on three occasions, nothing had been done.

Threats of violence were extremely intimidating, a few callers had been threatened with knives and pellet guns. A group of children found that the assaults or threats followed them home – they had their windows broken, abusive phone calls, racist anonymous letters, and racist abuse shouted through the letterbox or in the street. This was where racist bullying merged with street violence. Two children who were threatened with having their homes burned were very frightened. They knew that black families have, on occasion, been burned out.

Most children suffering bullying have their home as a place of refuge and respite. To feel threatened there too is very hard to bear.

Bullying and prejudice

A further group of youngsters, spoken to over the period studied, suffered xenophobic, class or homophobic bullying or that based on religious difference. Though these calls were not counted in the sample, it is worth comparing their experience with that of children suffering racist bullying.

Here children who moved country or region within the UK or from outside seemed vulnerable, as did children from families practising particular religions or being seen as very religious. A number of calls were from Scottish and English children who had moved country. One religious group seemed especially vulnerable to becoming a target: children from Jehovah's Witness families. Children from other minority religions seem to be much more likely to have racist than anti-religious comments made to them unless they are seen as particularly rigorous practitioners.

'I'm American and I moved to Scotland recently. I get lots of hassle. My parents tell me to ignore it, but I can't. Some nights I cry myself to sleep.'

'I'm a Jehovah's Witness. I'm the only one in the class. They call me names and it makes me cry. I can't help it. I told Mum and the teachers. They said to ignore it but that didn't work . . . It would be easier if I had just one friend. My parents are nice to me, but I get so lonely at school . . . I'm on crutches at the moment because one of the boys kicked me on the knee . . . How do you go about moving school?'

'I've been beaten up by a gang of girls at the Protestant school . . . I go to the Catholic one . . . Mum took me to the police and they've taken a case out against the gang . . . I'm so scared they will take revenge.'

It was clear that a similar process of scapegoating was at work here as in calls about racist bullying. A child or children were identified as being different, and rejected, enabling a group sense of cohesion or superiority. This process can be readily anticipated in any group where single children of different backgrounds join a largely heterogeneous group. It is then that teachers, youth leaders and parents can plan prevention. Where pronounced and long-standing communal or sectarian disturbances exist, single children on the streets are at risk and making the streets safer is vital.

Effects of racist bullying

It will be clear from the children's accounts that their lives were made miserable by the constant barrage of abuse and rejection.

Callers regularly described feelings of distress, anger and fear. Many were angry at themselves for 'letting it get to them' – as if that could be avoided. But this sense of dissatisfaction with themselves was often reinforced by the responses of adults when they asked for help. Children commonly described being advised to 'ignore' the bullying, or not to 'take it so seriously'.

Some callers were bunking off school at times. Others reported school work being affected. Headaches, stomach aches and nightmares were mentioned commonly. But the greatest impact was on their emotional well-being and their sense of identity.

They felt hated and they felt despised. These feelings were exacerbated by the sense that the views embodied in the harassment were widely held. It is extremely difficult to maintain a sense of self-worth against such relentless persecution as the children here described. So it was not surprising, though disquieting, to find that a number of youngsters described feelings of self-hatred and rejection of their colour or culture, and sometimes of their family or parents. These feelings brought their own shame.

'I don't like being black.'

'I'm ashamed of my Dad.'

'I hate my dad. He made me black.'

'I wish I was the same colour as them . . . it's awful because it's all my own fault.'

These responses in children emphasise the importance of positive images of black people, and of different ethnicities, religions and cultures as a counter to the overwhelming negativity which these children face.

It also suggests that it is essential but not enough to stop the racial harassment. Once children have suffered, attention needs to be paid to helping them recover their confidence and self-esteem.

Leroy, 11, told ChildLine he was off school until the new school year because he gets called racist names. He told his parents and the teachers. His parents went to the school but nothing changed. He ended up taking an overdose because the bullying became so bad. He was at home and safe now, but preoccupied about whether it would start again in the new class.

Nineteen of the callers described suicidal feelings or attempts. This was 4.4 per cent of the sample, a slightly higher rate than the 4 per cent found in the ChildLine study of bullying across the board (ChildLine, 1996).

● The above is an extract from *Children and Racism*, published by ChildLine. See page 39 for address details.

© ChildLine

Where ethnic mix proves no barrier to success

Headteacher relies on happy atmosphere and effective monitoring to provide encouragement

The head of Childwall School in Liverpool, which boasts that it is one of the most ethnically mixed in the city, prefers to talk in terms of individuals rather than ethnic groups.

'It's too easy a demarcation to say that one particular group is not doing well,' said Dewi Phillips, head for three years. 'It may be true in general terms, but I believe all pupils have to be treated on their merits and their potential maximised.

'I don't think ethnic origin is the dominant factor in academic performance. We have many children who come to us from homes which one might describe as disadvantaged in terms of support for homework and things like that. But we are able to raise the achievement of many of our children from all ethnic backgrounds.'

Good news spreads fast and many parents are now beginning to beat a path to Childwall's door. The school boasts no miracles but relies on good monitoring, effective counselling and relentless encouragement.

'We want children to understand the need for success and that message is sent home through letters and meetings to make sure parents understand what we are about. We explain how we will attempt to get the best out of every child. The message is repeated frequently at school.

'The ethos of the school is one of achievement in a happy and caring environment and in the last three or four years our exam results have improved dramatically.'

Ethnicity can be an issue because many at Childwall are bilingual and need special support. 'We are aware that there is a debate about the lower achievement of some

By David Ward

Afro-Caribbean children. But it's not the key issue. Here we try to ensure that each pupil gets an equal share of the available resources and staff are at pains to ensure that everyone has access to all parts of the curriculum.'

The ethos of the school is one of achievement in a happy and caring environment

The abilities of pupils in maths, reading and verbal reasoning are assessed when they enter the school and during their progress through it.

'Screening indicates if achievement is beginning to slip. Parents will be quickly informed. It's a question of knowing our children and knowing what they are capable of.'

Pupils with no family history of participation in higher education are told how to find their way to university. 'We have to open doors for them and we have a compact with John Moores University. We stress to pupils that the better qualified they are, the better position they are in to make something of their lives.

'I can't pretend for one minute that we achieve everything with all our children – and we have a hard core who do not attend very regularly – but we certainly like to think most get the best they can out of this school.'

© *The Guardian*
September, 1996

BLACK & WHITE BOARD

ST GOOD SCHOOL

KenPyne

Plight of a school shunned by whites

Like countless other headmistresses, Kay Lindley welcomes her pupils each day as their parents drop them at the school gate.

The difference is that her school is an entirely white area – yet almost all the youngsters are Asian.

Parents living within yards of Utley First School in Keighley, West Yorkshire, prefer to drive their children up to 12 miles away to virtually all-white schools. Some even cross into North Yorkshire.

Utley starkly illustrates the growing phenomenon of 'white flight' from schools by parents who have turned their back on liberal notions of multicultural education. They insist they are not racists, but simply do not want their children in schools where they feel a minority.

A confidential report by Bradford City Council warned that the exodus was affecting the provision of school places in Keighley – some schools had long waiting lists, while others with large Asian populations had empty places.

One Asian school governor, Khadim Hussain, said the racial divide was now 'reaching a par with apartheid'.

By all accounts, Utley is a good school, with a fine educational record, despite the fact that many pupils arrive not speaking any English.

Virtually all the pupils, aged five to nine, are from Showfields, an overwhelmingly Asian area about a mile away. Signs in the school are in English, Urdu and Punjabi, and even the school brochure is in English and Urdu.

This year there are four white children among the 100 pupils, but none is from the surrounding area.

Mrs Lindley does not like to say so, but believes the clear reason for their decision is racial prejudice.

By Tony Halpin, Education Correspondent

'Some parents have tried to couch it in all sorts of wonderful ways, but by and large they will say they are not happy with the mix in the school,' she said.

'They say if it was 50-50 they would be happy, but when I point out that it would be if their children stayed they are still not willing to do it.'

Stephen Lewis, 38, lives 250 yards away from Utley school, but drives his 6 year-old son Jordan 12 miles to East Morton Primary. He said: 'Any white child who went there would be in a minority.

'People here don't even entertain going to that school.'

© The Daily Mail
October, 1996

Education

Contrary to popular belief, white women are the least likely to have higher education qualifications. Twelve per cent have a higher qualification, compared with 13 per cent of women from ethnic minorities, and 15 per cent of white men. At the top of the table are men from ethnic minorities, 18 per cent of whom have higher education qualifications. But there is a great disparity between the level of education of the different ethnic groups. Over a third of black African women have a higher education qualification, compared with only 6 per cent of their Caribbean counterparts. And nearly a quarter of Chinese women have a higher education qualification, yet for Bangladeshi women the figure is only 3 per cent.
Sadly, unemployment is twice as high among black people with higher education qualifications (9 per cent) as it is among similarly qualified whites (4 per cent).

UK domiciled students by ethnicity 1995/96	
White	982,286
Black Caribbean	15,110
Black African	18,562
Black other	6,186
Indian	31,921
Pakistani	15,374
Bangladeshi	3,996
Chinese	8,458
Asian other	12,070
Other	16,499
Unknown	359,726
Grand total	**1,470,188**

1995 UCAS entries
Home admissions to full-time, first-degree courses by ethnicity and gender

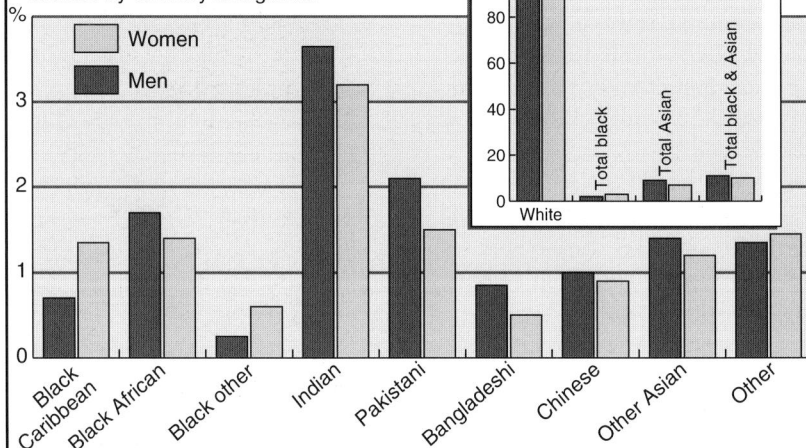

Source: IES Annual Graduate Review 1996-7

'My racist parents hate my boyfriend'

Jane, 17, has a secret boyfriend because of her parents' racist views . . .

Until two years ago I had no idea Mum and Dad would refuse to let me go out with a black guy. Then they saw me chatting with three black lads when they picked me up after a night out. I didn't think there was a problem, but when we got home, Dad was fuming.

Racist rant

He asked me what I thought I was doing talking to 'boys like that'. I did fancy one of the guys, Damien, but I said they were just friends because I could see Dad would freak out otherwise.

Mum and Dad kept saying they didn't have anything against black people, but felt mixed-race relationships were wrong. They said it wasn't fair on half-caste children. I thought it was crazy to talk about children – after all, I was only 15 – but Mum said if white lads saw me with black guys they wouldn't be interested in me!

I hit the roof. We had a blazing row, they got really angry, and I ended up in tears. In the end, they barred me from seeing the boys again. I went to bed feeling angry and hurt. I just couldn't understand it, as they had quite a few friends who weren't white and I've never heard them make racist remarks before.

At school the next day my friends could tell something had upset me, but I was too ashamed to tell anyone except my best friend. I was really embarrassed that my parents were so prejudiced.

I'm quite close to Mum and Dad and hated the bad atmosphere at home, so although I really liked Damien, I agreed not to meet him or his mates again. But it was weeks before they stopped interrogating me every time I went out.

After that I went out with a white guy, but it didn't last long.

Then three months ago I met Sean, who's 21, at a club. He's black too, so although I really liked him, I couldn't help thinking about Mum and Dad while we chatted.

Locked in a dilemma

When Sean asked to see me again, I took a while to say yes. I didn't want to go against my parents' wishes, but in the end I decided I couldn't pander to their prejudice for the rest of my life.

After a week, Sean asked why he couldn't pick me up from home. When I told him, he was really upset.

We go out about twice a week and really like each other, but we have to make sure no one sees us, and I can't tell my mates about Sean in case it gets back to Mum and Dad.

Fear of the truth

I feel really guilty about deceiving my parents because I've never lied to them before, but I'm scared of what they'd do. I don't think they'd kick me out, but I'm not certain.

I've promised Sean I'll tell Mum and Dad as soon as the time is right, but so far I haven't had the nerve. I wish they could see that it doesn't matter what colour Sean is, it's his personality that counts.

Advice

* Racists use religion and ethnic origin as excuses for hating people.

* It's hurtful to be insulted for being in an inter-racial relationship, and it's even worse when your family are the ones at fault.

* For help and advice, call Child-Line free on 0800 1111, or Careline on 0181-514 1177.

© Just Seventeen September, 1996

Youth against Racism in Europe

Youth against Racism in Europe (YRE) is an international youth organisation, active in 16 countries in Europe. YRE was launched by an international demonstration of 40,000 people against racism in Brussels, in October 1992. We keep in touch regularly with each other about what is happening in different countries and how we can build international campaigns against racism. In August 1994 we organised an anti-racist camp of 1,500 young people from all over Europe in Germany.

YRE believes that racism isn't natural; it is something that can be overcome through education and campaigning. Unemployment, homelessness and poverty can all be used to encourage racism by Nazis and politicians. Black and Asian people are a visible minority, and therefore can easily be used as a scapegoat for social and economic problems.

YRE therefore don't just say racism is wrong but use economic arguments to convince people that blacks and Asians are not to blame for these problems. We think that the economic system we live in creates poverty, unemployment and low wages. We campaign for the right to a job, a home and an education for all and show that we can fight for these things best by overcoming racism and uniting.

YRE also campaigns to drive Nazi groups out of our communities. Wherever they organise we will mobilise local people to oppose them – in order to prevent them from spreading their Nazi ideas and recruiting new members.

The YRE was part of the successful campaign to close the British National Party's headquarters in South-East London. We co-organised the two biggest national demonstrations of 8,000 and 50,000 which eventually succeeded in shutting it.

We are campaigning for justice for people who are unjustly imprisoned like Oliver Campbell, Winston Silcott and the M25 Three, who YRE believes are the victims of racist frame-ups.

> **We regularly visit schools to speak with the students about racism and fascism and what can be done about them**

We campaign against racist immigration laws, and the imprisonment of asylum-seekers. YRE takes up individual cases of people threatened with deportation and exposes the injustice of the present immigration system.

YRE members are against all forms of discrimination. We believe everyone should have equal rights whether they are Asian, black or white, male or female, disabled or able-bodied, Jewish or Gentile.

School student members of YRE are active in combating racism both inside and outside school. We regularly visit schools to speak with the students about racism and fascism and what can be done about them. There are YRE groups in a number of schools.

YRE is run and controlled by its members. We are also keen to work with other groups – from local community groups to national organisations and trade unions.

Young people of all races, Asian, black and white, must unite against racism. We are the ones who have most to lose from racism and fascism, and most to gain from their defeat. United we can win.

• The above is an extract from an *Anti-racist Education Pack*, published by Youth against Racism in Europe. See page 39 for address details.

© *Youth against Racism in Europe (YRE) 1996*

Beat it!

Racism can affect all our lives. Here's all the information you'll need to help stamp out the problem now!

Are you a victim?

Here's our 10-point plan to solving the problem . . .

1. Stop taking the abuse

You don't have to accept this sort of hassle. Everyone has a right to live happily and free from discrimination, no matter what their nationality, so do something now to make the situation better.

2. Accept that you're not the one with the problem

Your self-esteem may have taken a knock if you're having a hard time, but the thing you have to remember is that you are not the one to have caused the problem. If other people are ignorant, misinformed or just nasty, then that's not your fault.

3. Tell someone what's happening to you

You don't have to suffer in silence. Think who's the best person to talk to about what's happening. Schools, police and employers have a responsibility to protect you – tell them you want action now! Other parts of your life will suffer if you keep silent. If the problem is at school, your work will deteriorate, so what are you going to do – hide at home for the rest of your life? Speak up now before the problem takes over. Why not try having a word with a ChildLine counsellor first to rehearse what you would like to say?

4. Go for a team effort

Get other people involved in tackling the problem – perhaps you could start an anti-racism project or newsletter at your school or youth group and invite an anti-racist speaker along. Or set up a discussion group to talk about relevant issues and see what you can do to help in your area.

5. Make people take you seriously

If you are going to alert someone to the fact that you're being threatened, abused or bullied then do it properly. Hinting you're unhappy isn't enough. You have to be prepared to get across how much it is affecting your well-being.

6. Keep some evidence of what's happening (e.g. a diary of events)

This might be useful to show others that you need help. You may not be able to count on friends/neighbours/school or workmates to speak up, because often they do not want to get involved.

7. Plan what you would like to happen – now go for it!

Give yourself a goal to work towards by imagining what it would take to sort the problem. Now draw up a plan and start working out how you'll achieve your goal.

8. Make other parts of your life even better

Don't let racists ruin every area of your life. For example, if you're unhappy at school or work then make sure you make up for the bad times by enjoying yourself at home or with your friends. Of course, it can be difficult to stop worrying sometimes, but don't you deserve to be happy?

9. Keep safe and aware

You can't spend your life looking over your shoulder, but it pays to be aware of dangers. If you have been threatened or attacked, don't walk into dangerous situations. Stick with groups of friends and ignore threats rather than rising to the bait.

10. Never give up!

You might not be able to tackle racism by yourself. Seek out support, accept help and look forward to a bright future!
© MIZZ
July, 1996

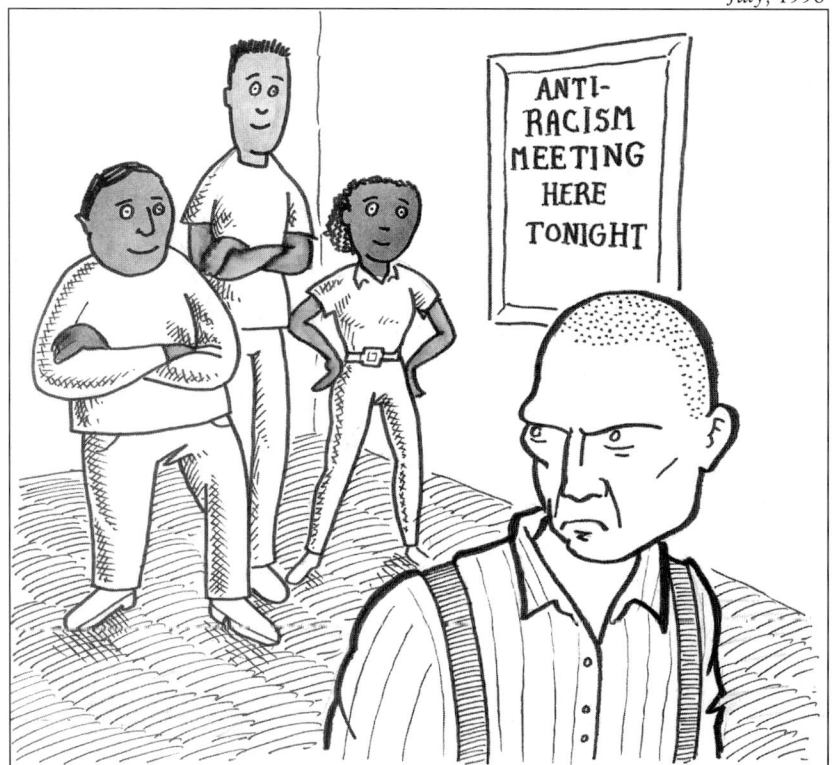

Racial attacks and harassment

What is racial harassment?

The Commission for Racial Equality (CRE) defines racial harassment as verbal or physical aggression towards individuals or groups because of their colour, race, nationality, or ethnic or national origin. It includes attacks on property as well as people.

Sources of data

Police records and the British Crime Survey (BCS) are the two main sources of information about racial incidents.

- The police are required to keep records of any incidents where a racial motive is apparent to the reporting or investigating officer, or is alleged by the victim.
  Police records cover *all* racial incidents reported to the police, whether they are criminal offences or not. They include incidents where white people are victims.
- The British Crime Survey, which was carried out in 1988, and again in 1992, included all crimes against South Asians (Indians, Pakistanis and Bangladeshis) and Black Caribbeans where a racial motive was alleged by the victim.
  The BCS was based on a sample of approximately 10,000 White households and 1,500 Black Caribbean and South Asian households. It did not ask other ethnic minorities, including White groups such as Jews or Irish people, about their experiences of racially motivated crime. The BCS conclusions are therefore based on a narrower range of incidents and victims than police records.

Levels of harassment

- The BCS estimated that in 1992 there were 130,000 racially

motivated crimes, with 89,000 against South Asians and 41,000 against Black Caribbeans.
However, as the figure of 130,000 is based on a relatively small sample, the number of incidents could be as high as 170,000 or as low as 90,000.

- This estimate of 130,000 would mean that 6% of all South Asians and 8% of Black Caribbeans had experienced racial harassment.
- About one in five of all incidents of criminal victimisation against someone from these groups was believed by the victim to be racially motivated.

Incidents reported to the police

Racial incidents are under-reported. However, the BCS found an increase in levels of reporting between 1988 and 1992.

- In 1992, the BCS calculated that 34% of racially motivated crimes were reported to the police by Black Caribbeans, compared with 27% in 1988. The level of crimes reported by South Asians rose from 39% in 1988 to 45% in 1992.
- The London Housing Survey estimated that over half (57%) of all racial incidents were reported to the authorities.
- In 1993 the number of racial incidents recorded by the police in England and Wales was 9,800, a rise of 27% from 7,700 in 1992.

Not all racial incidents are recorded as such by the police. This may be because the victim does not refer to the racial element, or because the police fail to note it.

Is it getting worse?

- In recent years the number of racial incidents reported to the

police has increased dramatically. From 1988 to 1993 the total for England and Wales more than doubled, as the figure opposite shows, with an increase of well over 50% in the London area.

- The rate of increase from 1988 to 1993 was twice as high in areas outside London as in London, with particularly high rates of increase in the figures reported for Cheshire, Derbyshire, Kent, and West Mercia.

This rise in recorded racial incidents may be due to an increase in reporting by victims, or an increase in recording by police when incidents appear racially motivated. The BCS provides no reliable evidence for an overall increase in the number of racially motivated crimes.

The geography of racial harassment

- Racial incidents and attacks are not spread evenly around Britain.
- In 1993, 40% of all racial incidents recorded by the police took place in the Metropolitan Police area. This may be partly because nearly half of Britain's ethnic minorities live in London.
- The other forces recording large numbers of incidents were Greater Manchester (658), West Midlands (487), Northumbria (405) and South Wales (400).
- In 1992, there were 663 racial incidents recorded by the police in Scotland. The force recording the highest number of incidents was Strathclyde, with 250 incidents.
- According to the BCS, half of all violent incidents in the street against Black Caribbean and South Asian people were seen as racially motivated. So were two-

thirds of all incidents against South Asians in and around their homes, and a quarter of the attacks on Black Caribbeans in pubs and clubs.

The victims

- The great majority of victims are members of non-white ethnic minority groups, with South Asians the most vulnerable.
- The BCS found that in inner-city areas, 18% of South Asians, 12% of Black Caribbeans and 5% of White people felt that racial attacks were a problem in their area.
- The London Housing Survey found that South Asian people with children living on housing estates were most at risk of racial harassment.
- Metropolitan Police figures show that South Asians are the largest group of victims (48%), followed by Black Caribbeans (24%) and White people (22%). Anti-Semitic incidents accounted for 8% of the total.
- White people, too, may be victims of racial harassment or violence, a point emphasised by a survey in Keighley which found that racial incidents were increasingly being reported by young White people.
- In 1993 the Metropolitan Police recorded that assaults made up 32% of racial incidents, criminal damage accounted for 30%, and abusive behaviour for 23%, with other offences making up the remainder.
- The Metropolitan Police's clear-up rate was 30%, an increase of 22% over 1992.

The offenders

- For incidents of racial violence and threats against Black Caribbean and South Asian victims, the BCS recorded that more than four out of five victims described the offender as White.
- Men were responsible for the majority (about 80%) of offences.
- 16–25 year-olds were responsible for over half the incidents against South Asians, and just over a third of those against Black Caribbeans.

- In about two-thirds of incidents the perpetrator was a stranger. South Asians were most likely to experience attacks or threats from groups of people, with nearly half these incidents involving groups of four or more.

The law

- Assaults of any sort are covered by the existing criminal law, but there is no specific offence of racial harassment in either civil or criminal law. However, a number of existing laws, both civil and criminal, can be used against perpetrators of these incidents. They include:
the Local Government Act 1972;
the Race Relations Act 1976;
the Public Order Act 1986;
the Malicious Communications Act 1988;
the Criminal Justice Act 1991.
- There has been a strong campaign to persuade the Government to give specific recognition to racial motivation in incidents of harassment and violence. Some, including the CRE, say that racial harassment should be a specific offence. Others say that existing laws are adequate. Whether judges should have a statutory duty to take racial motivation into account when passing sentence is also a matter of debate.

Community action

Local initiatives have had considerable success in combating racial attacks.

- An alarm scheme in Leicester has helped the police, the local authority and ethnic minority communities to join together against racial violence.
- In Dundee local residents from all communities successfully banded together to combat a rise in racial incidents on their housing estate.
- On the Cherry Gardens housing estate in Southwark, London, the local neighbourhood housing office took action against a gang of White young people who had been responsible for racist attacks, intimidation and criminal damage against Black and Asian families. The housing office took the case to court and got an injunction prohibiting ten of the core gang members from assembling in the area and from causing any further harassment to any council tenants. This positive action gained the London Borough of Southwark first place in the CRE Local Authority Race Awards for 1994.

© Commission for Racial Equality 1996

Racial incidents

Racial incidents reported to the police in England and Wales, 1988–1993

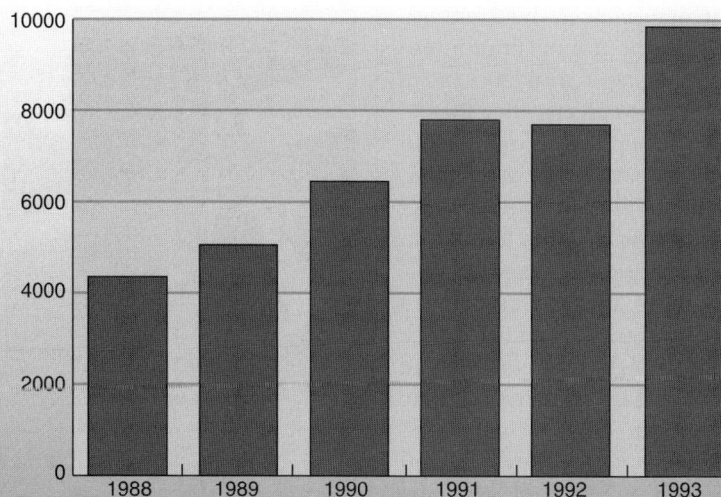

Source: Police Records 1988–1993

Facts about racism in Britain

Information from Cities in Schools

Racial discrimination

The Race Relations Act of 1976 makes it unlawful to discriminate against anyone because of their race, colour, nationality (including citizenship), ethnic or national origins. It applies to:

Jobs

Training

Housing

Education

Services – from councils, the health system, banks, pubs, clubs, restaurants, accommodation agencies etc.

There are two kinds of discrimination

Direct discrimination

This happens when someone is treated worse or differently to others because of their race, colour, nationality, or ethnic or national origins. For example, if an Asian woman does not get a job in a company because she won't 'fit in' with the staff who are all white, she has been directly discriminated against.

Indirect discrimination

This happens when everyone seems to be treated the same way, but because of certain conditions or requirements, one group of people are put at a greater disadvantage. This can be intentional or unintentional. For example, a Liverpool store manager told a careers office that he didn't want applicants from certain postal districts. These were areas where there was a high percentage of black residents. The law found him guilty of indirect discrimination.

Inciting racial hatred is a criminal offence, and includes: threatening behaviour, abuse and insults, as well as publishing anything that is likely to cause racial hatred.

Despite the law, racial discrimination, as well as racial harassment and violence, are still widespread, and run through all areas of society. The law cannot change, or do anything about, people's attitudes, particularly when institutionalised racism is not legally recognised. It is also often difficult to prove that discrimination is happening. In a survey called '*British Social Attitudes, the 1994 Report*', which interviewed a representative cross-section of people, 90% of those interviewed felt Britain was a racially prejudiced society, and 60% thought discrimination flourished.

Justice

A young black man is four times as likely to be arrested and twice as likely to be charged (rather than cautioned) as a young white man.

- November 1994 is the first time that police have released figures showing the 'racial' breakdown of people stopped and searched by them.

- Nearly half of all the people stopped and searched by some police forces are black; 42% in London even though only 8% of Londoners are black. The police denied that this was an indication of harassment and intimidation.

Bernie Grant, MP, said that some of the 'justifications' given for stopping and searching black people included:
a car's foglamps being on,
a driver taking a roundabout route,
a driver unlawfully displaying an L plate.

- 4.8% of the population are from black 'racial' groups – 23% of the total prison population are from black 'racial' groups.

- Complaints about racial discrimination and serious assault by police officers rose from 67 in 1992 to 291 in 1993.

- Out of 2,000 part-time judges serving the Crown Court and County Courts only 27 are black. In the permanent posts, only one out of 294 district judges is black. Out of 510 circuit judges only three are described as 'Asian' and one as 'non-European' (no other black 'racial' groups are represented). Almost all members of the judiciary are drawn from Oxbridge-educated males and the elitist membership of the Bar.

Employment

Black people are twice as likely to be unemployed as white people even when they are better qualified, because of discrimination by employers and organisations.

- Claims against employers on the grounds of racial discrimination have reached an unprecedented level according to the annual report of the Advisory Conciliation and Arbitration Service. During 1993, they received 1,850 complaints, 6% up on 1992.

Housing and homelessness

Black people are four times more likely to be homeless in London than whites. Additionally:

- One in five accommodation agencies discriminate against black people.
- 94% of white families, but only 57% of Bangladeshi and Pakistani families, have at least one room per person.

Racial violence

On average, a racial attack occurs every half hour. Black people are 60 times more likely than white people to be targets. Asian people, particularly women and children, experience the highest number of attacks.

- A 1994 report by the Home Affairs Select Committee on Racial Attacks and Harassment documents that the number of reported racial attacks rose from 4,383 in 1988 to 7,793 in 1992, an increase of 78%.
- The United Nations Human Rights Commission has condemned Britain for failing to do enough to halt the significant increase in racial incidents: over the last five years racial incidents have soared by over 50%. In November 1994, the Commission therefore announced that they would be carrying out a full investigation into racial discrimination and violence in Britain.
- The 1994 Anti-Semitism World Report documents a 20% rise in anti-Jewish attacks in the past year; including serious assaults, threats, the desecration of cemeteries and synagogues and the widespread distribution of anti-Semitic literature.
- Figures from the British Crime Survey estimate that the true number of racial attacks could be around 140,000 a year, meaning that only 1 in 16 are reported to the police.
- In an eight week study in Burley, Leeds, in 1994, Leeds University researchers recorded 84 incidents of racial harassment, ranging from verbal abuse and stone throwing to stabbings, all perpetrated by children. The average age of the culprits was seven.

Black and British

Records show that there have been black British people since at least the end of the 15th century.

- The first black Britons almost certainly came to Britain with the Romans, 2,000 years ago, long before the Angles or the Saxons arrived. Roman records refer to soldiers, described as 'Moors', from northern Africa, defending Hadrian's Wall. Ironically, this wall was built as a barrier to keep the Scots out of Britain.
- More than 50% of Britain's black population was born in Britain (1991 census analysis) and more than 75% are British citizens. Approximately 15% of white people were born outside Britain.

Health

Compulsory detention under the Mental Health Act is 25 times more likely for young black people aged 16–25 than for young white people aged 16–25.

- 1991 census analysis shows that black people face widespread discrimination in employment, access to housing and health services. This directly affects physical and mental health.
- Black and Irish children have higher rates of long-term illness than any other group, while young Bangladeshi adults are twice as likely to have long-term illnesses.

Education

Research by the Commission for Racial Equality in Birmingham, and further research all over the country, found that African-Caribbean pupils are four times as likely as white pupils to be suspended for the same kinds of misbehaviour.

- By law, state schools are compelled to have some form of daily Christian worship even though many pupils are of other religious denominations.
- In 1989, there were fewer than 20 black headteachers in all the schools in Britain.
- A 1994 study by Norwich and Norfolk Racial Equality Council, and previous research in the West Country and Wales, has revealed that whilst black people make up less than 1% of rural communities, almost all black people living in rural areas have experienced extreme racism: racial harassment, taunts, discrimination and violence. Primary as well as secondary school playgrounds produced some of the worst and most frequent examples of racism, and the research found that few schools are prepared to recognise it, let alone tackle it.
- An extensive research study at the Institute of Education, Warwick, in 1994, showed that black pupils, and African-Caribbean pupils in particular, are outperforming pupils of all other races at the age of five and stay in the lead until at least the age of seven.

By 16, African-Caribbean pupils are the least educationally successful, and many senior educationalists blame this on schools' low expectations, stereotypical views and prejudice.

Anti-racist organisations

There are many organisations, both locally and nationally, who are actively fighting against all forms of racial discrimination.

The Commission for Racial Equality exists to enforce the Race Relations Act, and will help anyone who feels they have been discriminated against.

- The above is an extract from *Challenging Racism, Valuing Difference – The Activities Book*, published by Cities in Schools – Tower Hamlets. See page 39 for address details.

© Cities in Schools – Tower Hamlets 1995

What the racists say

Information from Youth against Racism in Europe

What the racists say:
'Blacks and Asians come to our country and steal our jobs,'
This is a racist lie

Racist groups claim that it is possible to get rid of unemployment by stopping immigration and 'sending foreigners usually Blacks and Asians back where they came from'.

- 8.1% of the working population of Britain is officially unemployed; only 5% of the total population is Black or Asian.
- Most immigrants to Britain are white. Around 40% of foreign-born workers in Britain are European Union nationals. Over half the people given work permits to work in Britain in 1994 were from the USA.
- Immigration to Britain is one of the lowest in Europe – since 1981 the number of people who have been accepted for settlement in Britain has stayed at the same level: between 50,000 and 60,000 per year.
- More people leave Britain than come in. For example, during the 1980s, 6,000 more people emigrated out of Britain than entered the country. The 1950s is the longest period this century where there have been more people entering Britain than leaving, but this only adds up to a net immigration to Britain of 12,000 over the whole 10 years. In 1992, 11,000 more people left Britain than entered. Today, well over 200,000 Britons live in other European Union countries.
- It isn't immigration which causes unemployment but lack of jobs. Sharp rises in unemployment are caused by changes in the economy – usually job losses in a recession – not because more people are coming into Britain. Some of the lowest unemployment Britain has

had this century was in the 1950s, when immigration into Britain was at its highest level since the Second World War.

- Black and Asian people are more likely to be unemployed than whites, even if they are highly qualified.
- Only one in four young Blacks leaving Youth Training schemes get jobs. This compares to one in three young disabled people and one out of two young whites.
- One out of every five Asian shopkeepers has a university degree; they were forced to open their own small businesses due to racial discrimination by employers.
- Black workers tend to have lower-paid and less secure jobs than their white counterparts. Even with employers who have an equal opportunities policy, Black and Asian people often find they are stuck in the lower grades with little chance of promotion.
- Many Black and Asian people in Britain today originally came here because they were asked to come and work by the British Government in the 1940s and 1950s. The British economy was expanding and the Government wanted extra workers, especially in lower-paid and labouring jobs where white people often weren't prepared to work. Government officials went to the West Indies to persuade people to come and work in Britain to reduce the labour shortage. A few years later when the labour shortage was no longer a problem, the same politicians who had supported immigration to provide extra workers for industry, began to call for an end to Black and Asian immigration and use racist arguments.

What the racists say:
'If it wasn't for immigrants getting priority for housing, less British people would be homeless.'
This is a racist lie

In Tower Hamlets, one of the reasons Derek Beackon got elected as a BNP candidate was his claim that Bengalis were taking all the houses and causing homelessness among white people. This is a racist lie:

- Black and Asian people are two and a half times more likely than white people to be made homeless.
- One in five housing agencies discriminates against ethnic minorities.
- Studies have shown that local authorities and housing agencies tend to house Black and Asian people in certain areas, no matter where they want to live: usually these are the most run-down, deprived estates with the worst housing.
- Black and Asian people are more likely to live in crowded, damp accommodation in poorer areas than whites.
- Shelter, the homelessness charity, estimates that there are 2,000,000 homeless people in Britain who aren't registered by any local authority. Yet in 1993, local authorities in Britain only started building 2,795 homes.
- No one needs to be homeless. Shelter estimates that 100,000 are needed every year to cope with the demand for housing. There are 830,000 empty homes in England. Seventeen thousand of these are owned by Government departments, and 700,000 by the private sector (up from 541,000 in 1983).
- Building homes, repairing housing which is unfit for living in and converting empty offices

to homes for people to live in would not only reduce homelessness. It would also create work and so reduce unemployment.

What the racists say:
'Foreigners are responsible for all the crime.'
This is a racist lie
Racist groups like the BNP try to spread the idea that Black people are 'natural' criminals and are responsible for the majority of crimes – especially violent ones like rape and muggings.

- The majority of rapes are committed by someone the rape victim knows well – often family.
- In areas like Newcastle and Glasgow, where there is a lot of poverty but very small Black and Asian populations, there aren't any fewer muggings – the vast majority of muggers are white.
- Studies have shown that there is a strong link between deprivation and crime such as burglary and mugging – that is, many criminals are forced into crime by their own personal circumstances and the general economic situation. If someone can't get a regular job with reasonable pay and doesn't have enough money to live on, they are more likely to turn to crime.
- Black and Asian people are more at risk than the white community from most types of crime. Three times as many Blacks and Asians are victims of muggings as white people; twice as many Black and Asian families suffer from burglaries.

Sources
CSO quoted in the *Financial Times* 5/8/95, 1991 Census, *Divided by Degrees* report by the GMB 1993, Department of Employment survey quoted in the *Observer* 12/2/95, *Black and Betrayed* report by the TUC October 1995, *Black Workers and the Labour Market* report by the TUC May 1995, *Social Trends 1995*, Labour Research, Commission for Racial Equality, British Crime Survey/Home Office, Shelter/Office of Population Censuses and Surveys (OPCS), *Homes still wasted* report by the Empty Homes Agency November 1995, Shelter.

© Youth against Racism in Europe

Fact or myth?

MYTH
THE BLACK POPULATION IS MANY MILLIONS.
FACT
THE BLACK POPULATION IS ESTIMATED TO BE 1¼ MILLION.
Only 3.2% of the population.

MYTH
WHITE PEOPLE ARE LEAVING BRITAIN AND BEING REPLACED BY BLACKS.
FACT
TWO WHITE PEOPLE COME TO BRITAIN FOR EVERY BLACK.

MYTH
THE BLACKS CAN ALL BE SENT BACK HOME!
FACT
40% OF OUR BLACK POPULATION WERE BORN HERE.
Home is Britain!

MYTH
IMMIGRATION IS MAKING BRITAIN OVERCROWDED.
FACT
SINCE 1964 MORE PEOPLE HAVE LEFT BRITAIN EACH YEAR THAN HAVE ENTERED.
Holland, Belgium and West Germany have more people per square mile than the U.K.

MYTH
THEY COME HERE AND TAKE OUR JOBS.
FACT
MANY VITAL SERVICES WOULD GRIND TO A HALT WITHOUT THEIR BLACK EMPLOYEES.

MYTH
IMMIGRANTS ARE RUNNING DOWN OUR INNER CITY AREAS.
FACT
BAD HOUSING CONDITIONS EXISTED LONG BEFORE BLACK IMMIGRANTS.
Urban decay has existed in Britain since the Industrial Revolution.

CRE admits Britain has good record on race

By James Meikle,
Community Affairs Editor

Britain's race relations record is among the best in Europe despite concerns about deepening alienation among some young ethnic minority groups, the Commission for Racial Equality (CRE) said yesterday.

A more upbeat message welcoming positive shifts in behaviour and attitudes, heralded in its annual report yesterday, is to be followed next month by publicity about the contribution black, Asian and Irish communities make to institutions and professions: London Underground, the National Health Service, the corner shop, university professorships and physicists.

But commission chairman Herman Ouseley warned against complacency and called for continuing 'hard graft' and leadership from public figures, adding that much discrimination was covert and subtle.

Half of Britain's black and Asian communities had been born here, and 'we ignore at our peril' the expectations of young people who wanted to be valued 'as black or Asian and British'. Their alienation had helped cause last year's 'skirmishes' in many parts of the country.

'Thankfully there were no major riots, but Bradford and Brixton came close . . . giving us a glimpse of the kind of social unrest none of us wants.'

Mr Ouseley suggested that asylum legislation – and newspaper coverage of it – did not match the Government's claim that 'fair but firm' race relations policies were in the best interests of all citizens.

'The notion of "bogus" arrivals at British airports has taken root in our folklore, and every message reinforces the damaging and false stereotype of immigrants as people who only know a few words of English: benefits, asylum and lottery handouts.'

This combined with images which suggested that all illegal immigrants and asylum seekers were people with African, Caribbean or Asian origins and 'it is little wonder that race relations are sometimes on a knife-edge'.

> *Formal applications to the commission for help in pursuing race discrimination cases fell from a record 1,937 in 1994 to 1,682 last year*

But Mr Ouseley added: 'We were able to draw some comfort from the knowledge that race relations in Britain during 1995 were as good as, if not better than, anywhere else in Europe, where intolerance and xenophobia have reached unacceptable levels... While we can give ourselves the occasional well-deserved, congratulatory pat on the back as a nation, we can and must do more to improve the present situation.'

Despite the positive signs of change, too many people still saw racism, discrimination and bigotry as someone else's problems.

Formal applications to the commission for help in pursuing race discrimination cases fell from a record 1,937 in 1994 to 1,682 last year, but previous dips in numbers have not lasted, and officials said it was difficult to monitor exactly how many cases were followed through other means.

Mr Ouseley appealed to the Home Office not to cut further its £15 million grant to the commission, which is £1 million down on last year's aid.

IT'S THE ONLY RACE WE'RE ANY GOOD IN

THE TIMES
football
cricket
Athletics
Tennis
etc

Ken Pyne

Black and white facts of modern romance

Race survey shows how one in three West Indian and African men are in mixed relationships

One in three black men is married to or living with a white woman, according to one of the most detailed surveys ever compiled on Britain's ethnic minorities.

The younger the couple, the greater the chance that they are from mixed backgrounds – with 40 per cent of black men aged 16 to 34 now in this kind of relationship. Only half as many black women have white partners.

Inter-racial relationships between people from different ethnic minorities – such as an Indian man with a black Caribbean woman – are extremely rare.

Working-class blacks are more likely to be in a mixed relationship than any other group, though it is less likely to lead to marriage.

The findings are contained in a report which provides a fascinating picture of the lifestyles and attitudes of Britain's 3.2 million ethnic population.

The report – published by the Office of National Statistics – concludes that the growth in mixed relationships is leading to a 'blurring' of 'the separate identities of ethnic groups'.

Commenting yesterday on why black men and white women were increasingly getting together, one psychologist, Anu Sayal-Bennett, said: 'We live in a multi-cultural society and that will be playing a major part.

'It could be an internalised racism on the part of black men – thinking that black women are not good enough. They could see it as an ego trip to have a pretty white blonde on their arm.

'For white women, there could be a bit of mystery. I think it is a myth about black male sexuality – sex would not be enough to sustain a marriage.'

By Jason Burt and Helen Carroll

Other experts have claimed that there could be an element of 'rebellion' by the white women who turn their backs on society's norms.

The survey has been compiled from 13 different sources, including the 1991 census, which was the first to include a question on race.

Inter-racial relationships between people from different ethnic minorities – such as an Indian man with a black Caribbean woman – are extremely rare

It shows that people from ethnic minorities are less likely to be in work, are paid less when they are and depend more on social security benefits.

Blacks, South Asians – Indians, Pakistanis and Bangladeshis – and other ethnic groups, such as Chinese, are also more likely to live in areas blighted by crime and be dissatisfied with their homes.

They take less exercise than the general population and are more susceptible to ill-health. While they drink less alcohol, they are far less worried about the effects of smoking.

The report shows huge distinctions between the various ethnic groups.

Editor Carol Summerfield said: 'There are often bigger differences between the various ethnic minority groups than between the ethnic minority population as a whole and the white population.'

However, the report also suggests that differences are becoming less obvious as more people from ethnic minorities are born in Britain.

The survey shows that 45 per cent of the ethnic minorities

population is in the Greater London area, with 25 per cent of all Bangladeshis living in Tower Hamlets. In Leicester, 20 per cent of all people are Indian.

Indians, Pakistanis and Bangladeshis have the biggest households – five people in the case of Bangladeshis, twice the size of the black and white households.

About half of black Caribbean children live with a lone mother.

'In their eyes you can see the uneasiness'

Jo-Ann Goodwin, 33, a freelance journalist and writer, met dancer Gilmar Cruz Silva, 28, at a nightclub. They have been married for a year.

She says: 'Before I met Gilmar I'd gone out with a Scottish presbyterian and it was perhaps because Gilmar was so different that I was attracted to him.

'I feel slightly uneasy walking down the street with him, or taking public transport. There is a flicker of uneasiness in white men's eyes partly because black men with white women is one of the last great sexual taboos. On the other hand, at parties I've been ignored by black women.

'I am worried about our future children being the target of racism because it's not something that I grew up experiencing, which makes it harder for me to know how to help them.'

He says: 'I think Jo-Ann is more anxious about possible racist tension than I am. She picks up on more than I do. I think she's also more attuned to listen for it.

'Ironically I receive more racism from Brazilian people than I do from native British.'

'Prejudice is far worse abroad'

Nancy Davey, 39, a local council administrator, met her partner Ben Nyeke, a newsagent, 20 years ago. They have two children, Natasha, nine, and Luke, six.

She says: 'Our relationship developed out of friendship. We had been living in bedsits in the same house for several months when we finally got it together.

'I liked him as a person and, although all of us living in the house were friends, we got on particularly well and found we had a lot in common.

'I was attracted to him physically as well. The old cliché about black men and their sexual prowess is simply not true – it would be no basis for a long-lasting relationship anyway.

'My family didn't have any problems with the fact Ben was black. We've had problems with racists but that was when we were living in Zimbabwe for a year.

'People there, black and white, found it very difficult coming to terms with the idea that we were an item.

'Once when Ben was in the supermarket a member of staff told him to carry the shopping out to his "madam's car".

'He thought it was quite funny but I was absolutely incensed.

'But it hasn't been a problem in Britain. Before the children went to school I was worried about what they might encounter but I don't think they have experienced any racist abuse. They go to a multi-cultural school so it may be different somewhere else.'

He says: 'She could have been black, Indian or Chinese – it wouldn't have made any difference to the way I felt about her.

'I suppose it begs the same question as with any other relationship: what does attract one person to another? It's a mystery to us all.

'We experienced racism in Zimbabwe, where I'm from originally, and from white South Africans when we visited Victoria Falls last Christmas. We were also abused when we were on holiday in Greece.

'But we've never had any problems in Britain. I wouldn't want to live anywhere else. I would never even want to visit America because I think we would have a much harder time of it there.

'The children haven't had any real problems and I certainly wouldn't expect it to be any worse for them than it is for black children in Britain.'

'Some people don't like it, but that's their problem'

Garth and Lorraine Ricketts married two years ago. He is a 34-year-old architect whose Jamaican parents came to Britain in 1959. She is 32 and runs a fashion shop. They live in London.

She says: 'Garth and I had been friends long before we started going out. We talked frankly about the problems we might encounter: both black and white people we knew took exception to the idea in principle, but we decided that was their problem, not ours. Some black people have asked me if it would not have been easier if I had married a white man. Estate agents were more helpful when I was house-hunting on my own than when I was with Garth.

'I think a lot of the old attitudes are dying out but they still persist in some quarters. However, I try not to let that bother me and just get on with my life with the man I love.'

He says: 'For an easy life and society's approval, a black girl would have been a sensible option, but you can't choose who you love.

'A lot of black people do not approve of our relationship. White people are more careful about what they say but they still look at us disapprovingly. If anything, this has strengthened our marriage.

'We are aware that mixed-race children have particular pressures on them but that is something we will confront when the time comes.'

Crime and prisons

Black people form a higher proportion of prisoners than would be expected from their total numbers living in Britain.

This is particularly true of young black women, who make up 15 per cent of the female jail population.

More than half of all black prisoners are serving sentences of four years or more, and the most common crimes include robbery and drug offences.

But people from all the ethnic groups are much less likely to use drugs than whites, with only 6 per cent of Bangladeshis admitting ever to using them.

Black people are most likely to have been the victims of crime themselves. A quarter of black car owners had suffered theft and 13 per cent of black homes had been burgled – twice the proportion for Pakistani, Bangladeshi and white groups.

Asians are most in fear of 'racially-motivated' attacks and being burgled. Six in ten Indian women worry about being mugged compared with one in five whites.

Education

Blacks are the least successful academically, with just 21 per cent gaining five or more GCSEs in 1993.

This compares with a figure of 45 per cent for Indians and whites and 51 per cent for other Asians including Chinese.

However, a higher proportion of blacks and Indians stay in full-time education after the age of 16 than whites.

The gap widens as the students grow older. After 18, for example, only 38 per cent of whites continue their education compared with 65 per cent of Indians.

A higher proportion of blacks are mature students.

Asian students are more likely to aim for academic qualifications, rather than take vocational courses.

Ethnic minorities generally prefer to study for degrees in science and medicine rather than languages or arts.

And Indians are twice as likely as all other groups to succeed.

Money matters

Indian men are the most likely to be in work and earn more than people from all other ethnic minorities.

Bangladeshis earn the least. Unemployment is most common among young blacks, Pakistanis and Bangladeshis – about 40 per cent compared with 23 per cent for young Indians and 14 per cent for young whites.

Pakistanis and Bangladeshis are more likely to work for themselves, but they are also more involved in part-time employment.

Consequently, these groups depend more on social security benefits, with less than half the income for their households coming from wages.

Among all ethnic households, few have savings and they are less likely than others to have a pension or invest in shares or Premium Bonds.

Hotel and restaurant work is most common among Asians. Blacks tend to be employed in education, health and the civil service.

Buying or renting

Blacks and Bangladeshis are more likely to rent, either privately or from a council, with the majority living in flats.

More Indians have bought their own homes. Experts believe that often this has been influenced by their desire to live close to the rest of their family.

Almost half of all Bangladeshi households suffer from overcrowding compared with just 2 per cent of white families.

While more than half of all white families live in places built after 1944, the majority of Pakistanis live in homes built before 1919.

This means they are saddled with bigger repair bills and are less likely to have central heating or double glazing.

Pakistanis are also the most dissatisfied with the place where they live. Only Indians, out of all the ethnic groups, tend to be happy.

Ethnic minority households are more likely to be in debt, with one in ten blacks behind with their mortgage payments.

© *The Daily Mail*
August, 1996

Football racism

The facts

Did you know?

Almost a quarter of professional footballers in Britain are black.

- There have been only a handful of Asian professional footballers in Britain, ever, although there are now more than 300 Asian football teams around the country. With more and more Asian clubs producing good-quality players, it can only be a matter of time!
- It's against the law to chant racist slogans at matches, but there's nothing that can be done to prosecute racists if they are shouting alone. To be against the law, more than one person has to join in the chant.
- Only about 1% of fans who go to

football matches come from ethnic minority groups.
- Professional players in Holland once went on strike to protest against racism in the game. Others in Italy, Germany and Britain have spoken out too.

Incidents of racism in football

Manchester United's Eric Cantona served a nine-month ban after his infamous kung fu kick on a racially abusive Crystal Palace fan in January 1995. John Barnes, who has also suffered racism, later commented, 'It's ironic that we are now talking about an issue involving a white Frenchman, but the fact is that racism has not gone away as completely as people might think.'

A riot at the Republic of Ireland versus England international in February 1995 resulted in the arrest of 41 English supporters and three Irish fans. About 40 people were injured. A racist skinhead group called Combat 18 were believed to have been responsible for much of the trouble. A member of the gang was arrested travelling to an England international in Norway eight months later.

Black policeman Floyd Higginson needed hospital treatment after being the victim of a racist attack when playing for a Sunday league side. He also suffered racist taunts and abuse about his job. The match he was playing in had to be abandoned when the player who fouled Higginson was sent off and trouble started.

West Ham United found themselves in hot water last year when their official programme described Spurs fans as 'yiddos' – a slang term used to describe Tottenham's Jewish followers. They made a full apology to players and supporters.

Aston Villa keeper Mark Bosnich was faced with police and FA action after making a Nazi salute to Spurs supporters in October 1996. He said it was just a joke, an imitation of Basil Fawlty, rather than a slur against Jewish fans.

Cyrille Regis, who played for England and West Bromwich Albion in the early 1980s, was sent a bullet through the post by an England fan, who was angry because Regis had been picked as one of the first black players to represent his country. The letter said, 'Step onto the Wembley turf and you'll get one of these through your knees', but Regis wasn't deterred from making his England debut.

What the players say . . .
Les Ferdinand
'When I hear racial abuse it spurs me on to go on and score goals but after the game it makes you think. Most of the sides are now carrying black players and people are shouting racist taunts and they have black players in their own sides. It's like "he's alright because he's our black" – you just can't understand it. Racism is not a football problem, it's a social problem. The more people who stand up and be counted the better.'

David Platt
'In the past there were a lot of things happening, like bananas being thrown on the pitch and so on. I wouldn't say it was just our problem, though. When I went to Italy I played in a game at Napoli and Julio Cesar the Brazilian defender was being stretchered off when one of the stretcher-bearers dropped him because he'd been hit on the head by a banana thrown by the Napoli fans. The proper supporters, the ones who go to watch football, don't discriminate between black and white players.'

Paul Ince
'I remember when I first started my career when I was 18 and my debut for West Ham was away at Newcastle and we lost 4-0. I was a sub and when I warmed up I got so much racial abuse.

'That's a long time ago, obviously, and I am not pointing the finger at Newcastle, but things have changed a lot since then. Seven or eight years ago it was very, very bad.

'I believe now the FA, the Football League and everyone has done so much to stop it. When I was playing in Manchester I didn't get any racial problems at all.'

Recognise a racist
Chants
Racists are the ones singing songs that have got nothing to do with skill, results or even who ate all the pies. They'd much rather put their nasty (and dangerous) racist comments across in a song.

Jokes
'It's only a laugh innit?' Yeah, they might seem harmless or funny at the time, but think about the players or fans who are the butt of the jokes for no reasons other than their colour, background or religion. How funny is it for them? And you are giving your seal of approval if you laugh.

Comments and abuse
It's easy to get carried away at a game and feel like you really do hate the ref, or an opposing player, or one of your own team who's messed up. But racists think colour, nationality and religion are also good reasons to give someone grief. What have they got to do with the game?

Ignorance
Racists use stereotypes and sweeping generalisations to get their warped points of view across. So they think it would be great if those foreigners and blacks went home again? But think – what sort of state would football be in if that *were* to happen? ©*Kick It Out*

How much do you know?

Try our quick quiz and suss out how much you know about the contribution of ethnic minority players to British football . . .

1. What percentage of professional players in Britain are black?
a. 15%
b. 20%
c. 25%

2. When did black players first start to play in British league football?
a. Around 1912
b. Around 1888
c. Around 1956

3. When John Parris was capped for Wales in 1932, he made history. Why?
a. He was the first black player to be capped for a national team in Britain.
b. He was the first player to be capped for a national team while under the age of 18.
c. He was the only black footballer playing in Britain at the time.

4. Who was the first black player to be capped for England?
a. John Barnes
b. Viv Anderson
c. Cyrile Regis

5. Why was Paul Ince a groundbreaker for black football players?
a. He was first to captain his team
b. He was first to captain the English national squad
c. He was the first player to challenge racism in the game

Answers: Take a point for each question scored correctly
1c, 2b, 3a, 4b, 5b.

More race attacks reported to police

By Alan Travis,
Home Affairs Editor

Reports to the police of racial attacks and intimidation are rising at a rate of 8 per cent a year, according to figures published by the Home Office.

The figures suggest the real level of racial attacks is rising for the first time since 1986, when the police started keeping separate figures on racially motivated incidents.

Until now ministers have insisted the rapid year-on-year increase in the number of racial attacks has been a reflection of the fact that the police were taking such incidents more seriously, and so victims were more prepared to come forward.

The Home Office figures show 11,878 racial incidents were reported to the police in the year to March 1995, compared with 10,997 in the previous 12 months. The British Crime Survey, which is based on interviews with victims, suggests that there are in fact as many as 130,000 racially motivated incidents, including graffiti and verbal abuse, every year.

Publication of the figures coincides with the opening of the private prosecution at the Old Bailey next Tuesday by the family of 18-year-old black schoolboy, Stephen Lawrence, who was stabbed to death at a south London bus stop in April 1993. His family have so far raised £66,000 from wellwishers to finance the prosecution.

The sharpest rises in the official figures were seen in the Northumbria police area, which includes New-castle, in South Wales, and in Derbyshire, all of which recorded increases of more than 20 per cent. The largest fall, of more than 30 per cent, was recorded in the West Midlands, where the number of recorded attacks dropped from 487 to 375.

The shadow home secretary, Jack Straw, said the figures showed that race was a significant motive in an increasing number of crimes.

'The change in report practices is only part of the explanation,' he said. 'The fact that the numbers are rising underlines our commitment to strengthen the law on racial harassment and racial attacks.'

The figures for 1994/95 do not reflect the introduction of a new offence of intentional harassment in February last year, which was intended to strengthen the law to deal with serious cases of persistent harassment. Mr Straw said it was important that the law specifically recognised racial harassment as a crime.

Police stop-and-search figures show 37 per cent of those stopped on the streets of London were members of ethnic minority groups despite the fact that they made up only 20 per cent of the capital's population.

Mr Straw said the aggravation of community relations caused by the disproportionate number of black and Asian people stopped by police would not be resolved until there were more officers from ethnic minorities.

© The Guardian
April, 1996

Violence round the country

Reported racial incidents (Selected forces)	1993/94	1994/5
Derbyshire	221	291
Hampshire	212	210
Lancashire	262	222
Leicestershire	315	366
Greater Manchester	658	637
Metropolitan Police	5,124	5,480
Northumbria (Newcastle)	405	508
Nottinghamshire	264	259
South Wales	400	517
Sussex	214	247
West Midlands	487	375
West Yorkshire	244	254
England and Wales	10,997	11,878

Source: Home Office

Tackling racial harassment

How Neighbourhood Watch can help

We should all be working for a just society, where everyone has an equal chance to work, learn and live free from racial discrimination, and from the fear of racial violence. This article looks at how Neighbourhood Watch can help tackle the incidence of racial harassment in your area.

What is racial harassment?

Racial harassment is violence which may be verbal or physical and which includes attacks on property as well as the person. It is suffered by individuals or groups because of their colour, race, nationality, or ethnic or national origins. It is suffered when the victim believes that the perpetrator was acting on racial grounds or there is evidence of racism. It includes racial 'jokes', snide remarks and name-calling as well as more serious assaults and persistent abuse.

The extent of racial harassment

On a local level, a MORI survey in Manchester examined the nature and extent of racial harassment and racially motivated crime. The survey was conducted on behalf of Manchester Safer Cities, managed by Crime Concern, in conjunction with Manchester City Council, Greater Manchester Police.

The survey, taken from a sample of black and minority ethnic communities, revealed:

- Two in five of those surveyed had experienced a racial incident in the last twelve months.

- Half agreed people in their area were frightened about being racially harassed.

- Two in five agreed that their children were frequently harassed.

- Almost two-thirds had taken measures to avoid experiencing harassment or racially motivated crime – including avoiding particular streets or areas, fitting alarms and not going out alone after dark.

- The most common forms of harassment included: being treated unfairly or unfavourably because of colour, race or ethnicity, and verbal abuse from gangs or individuals.

- The most common experiences of racially motivated crime were damage to cars, burglary, and damage or vandalism to the home.

- Incidents were most often committed near the home, with some also taking place at work or on public transport.

- 71% of offenders were male and 66% were described as white.

- 81% of those who had experienced a racial incident had not reported it to the police.

- After a racial incident, victims were most likely to ask friends (90%) and family (88%) for support. 63% said they would approach the police, 39% said they would approach Victim Support or self-help groups, and 38% said they would approach the council or councillors.

The impact of racial harassment and racial violence

Racial harassment can be debilitating, both physically and emotionally. It can range from petty name-calling through to racial abuse, threats, vandalism and assaults. At its most extreme it can result in horrific violence; 3.6% of all racial incidents recorded by the police in 1995/96 involved serious physical violence.

Some examples of racial violence are given here.

Mohan Singh Kullar, a shopkeeper in Neath, West Glamorgan, was bludgeoned to death by a 22-year-old man, who had earlier told his friends what he thought of Pakistanis.

Ghanaian Osman Chan, playing in a charity seven-a-side match in Penrith, was attacked with a broken glass bottle when he protested to a man who was hurling racial abuse at him and making monkey noises from the touchline.

In London, a Jewish family who had suffered years of racial abuse from their neighbours, after a dispute over a garden fence, were awarded damages of £8,000. The judge granted an injunction against one of the neighbours, who also had to pay the costs of the case, estimated at £25,000.

Three black teenagers punched and kicked a man into a coma outside a nightclub in Nottingham, chanting racial abuse all the while. The judge jailed them for a total of 35 years and said he was imposing long sentences because of the racist element in the attack, and as a deterrent to other gangs 'prowling the streets'.

In Stirlingshire, two men in their twenties were jailed for attempting to murder seven people when they firebombed an Asian family home.

Mukhtar Ahmed was attacked in East London by a gang of about twenty youths. He nearly died after being so severely kicked that his scalp was detached from his skull. One man was given a two-year sentence: he was prosecuted because his girlfriend spoke out about the attack.

In South Wales, Ian Gibbs was stabbed to death because he defended staff at an Indian take-away who were being abused by a youth.

In South London, 15-year-old Rolan Adams was killed by a gang of white youths on his way home. When Orville Blair was later stabbed on the same estate, white youths roamed the streets chanting 'two-nil'.

What action can you expect others to take?

The police have a role to play in protecting, helping and reassuring the community; this will play a valuable part when dealing with racially motivated incidents. The police also have responsibility for recording and monitoring racial incidents. Racial incidents that are also criminal should be investigated as usual, including visits to the victim, taking statements and gathering evidence. If there is sufficient evidence, details should be passed to the Crown Prosecution Service, which will decide whether to prosecute or not.

Public and social housing providers have a responsibility to ensure that tenants are not harassed. If tenants are found to be racially harassing others, providers may use a wide range of laws as remedies, including enforcement of tenancy agreements where appropriate.

Education authorities and schools are able to help too, as they have a duty to take effective action against racial harassment, attacks or racial bullying, both in school and on the way to school.

Health services have a responsibility to recognise and respond to the physical and emotional needs of a person who has been racially attacked or harassed. This includes examining the degree of shock or trauma suffered, and arranging suitable treatment, including long-term counselling.

Social services departments are able to help victims cope with the abuse and distress of harassment.

Employers have a responsibility to protect and safeguard their employees from racial harassment by other employees, customers or clients. Racial harassment should be treated as a disciplinary offence.

How can Neighbourhood Watch Co-ordinators help?

Racial harassment is a particularly damaging crime. We all have a responsibility to ensure that no form of racial harassment goes unchallenged in our neighbourhood.

As a Neighbourhood Watch Co-ordinator you have an important role to play.

- Check that your Neighbourhood Watch includes everyone, and encourages people from ethnic minorities to join.

- Check with local people from ethnic minorities if they have been abused or harassed, and encourage them to report it to the police if they haven't already done so.

- If you witness a racial attack, inform the police.

- Get the local council involved.

- Find out if there is a Racial Equality Council or local support group to help victims of racial incidents.

- If children are affected by racial incidents, report their experiences to the headteacher and the education authority.

- Ask for the matter to be raised in the appropriate consultative forum, such as: police and community liaison committees, crime prevention panels and community safety partnerships.

- Keep leaflets on the issue and a list of useful contacts available for Neighbourhood Watch members.

- Conduct a 'fear of crime' survey in your area.

© *Taken from a Neighbourhood Watch publication produced in conjunction with Crime Concern and the Commission for Racial Equality.*

Double whammy for minorities struggling to find work

Unemployment: ethnic jobless rate nearly double normal because of racial discrimination in Scotland

The spirit of racism may be dying in South Africa, but in Scotland's labour market it appears to be alive and kicking.

Research among black and ethnic minority residents on one of Edinburgh's housing schemes has discovered that a staggering 60 per cent of active adults are unemployed – more than three times the local average of 19.3 per cent, double the national average.

It is an extreme example, but not uncharacteristic of Scotland as a whole, according to the Commission for Racial Equality, which is seeing a growing gap in black and white employment prospects reflected across the nation.

'In Scotland, as in the rest of the UK, the black unemployment rate is getting on for double the rate of white unemployment, and on peripheral estates and in run-down areas of city centres these problems are magnified,' says Mick Conboy, policy officer for the CRE in Scotland.

The discrepancy is echoed by the latest statistics from the Department of Employment, which put white joblessness in the UK at 7.7 per cent, but ethnic minority unemployment at 17.6 per cent.

The future could be even worse, judging by last summer's figures for school-leavers, which showed that unemployment for white youths aged 16 to 24 stood at 15.8 per cent as against 35.2 per cent for their ethnic minority counterparts. But the problem does not appear to be lack of qualifications or skills. Out of 57 people interviewed in the survey, which was conducted by the Wester Hailes Against Racism Project (WHARP), more than 65 per cent had standard-level qualifications or

By Nick Thorpe

higher, and nearly 42 per cent had degrees.

'The bottom line is discrimination on racial grounds,' says Conboy. He cites the preliminary results of an as-yet-unpublished CRE investigation in which identically qualified black and white applicants applied for a range of jobs in cities including Edinburgh and Glasgow – and discovered what appeared to be blatant breaches of race relations law.

'At one fairly reputable organisation the white candidate was told to fill in an application form, while the black candidate was told: "I'm sorry, there's nothing available at the moment," he recounts.

He believes it is a typical scenario, and one which requires a concerted Government response if the race gap is not to become bitterly entrenched.

'Without being alarmist, if young people continue to be cut off from participating in society they will find other ways of expressing their frustration,' he says.

That frustration was evident in responses to the WHARP survey, even among those who found jobs. One black man, a qualified vet, reported filling in more than 100 application forms before settling for part-time clerical work. 'The jobs advertised in the Job Centre are bogus,' wrote another jobseeker. 'I know that if I apply for 20 jobs I will not get any of them. It seems like the system is wrong.'

Unemployment rates

Averages for June 1995 – May 1996 (%)
Working age: 16–59/64 years

	All	Men	Women
All groups	9	10	7
White	8	9	6
Non-white	18	20	16
Black Caribbean	19	22	16
Black African	28	27	29
Black other	20	*	21*
Black mixed	22	*	*
Indian	12	13	11
Pakistani	26	26	25
Bangladeshi	33	26	*
Chinese	*	*	*
Other	15	17	11

* Numbers under 6,000; estimates not included

Source: Labour Force Survey

Such concerns are, of course, also true for white jobless people. But ethnic minorities can suffer twice, not only from their own soaring unemployment, but from the kick-back effect of joblessness in the general community, where boredom can spawn racial harassment.

'Young unemployed white people need to be rounded up and given some form of forced employment, which will give them less time to racially harass us,' said one frustrated resident, who, like others, was afraid to give his name for fear of recriminations. Nearly 60 per cent of those questioned said they had suffered some kind of racial harassment, with physical violence in the case of 17 per cent.

'Everywhere we have been in Scotland it is the same,' said a Middle Eastern woman whose husband, a qualified engineer, was beaten with a stick and told to 'go back to your own country', as he came home from his part-time teaching job late at night.

'At our last house people threw stones through our windows, went to the toilet outside our door, and set a dog on me. Now we would like to move again. I do not understand why they do this to us.'

Milind Kolhatkar, the chairman of Wester Hailes Against Racism Project, believes the answer to unemployment lies in 'positive action' training programmes to help black or ethnic minority applicants to combat the bias in the system.

And if that means accusations of positive discrimination, so be it, according to Selma Rahman, the chairwoman of Skillnet, Scotland's first employment and training project for black and Asian people.

Launched last month and funded by Urban Aid, the project offers a 12-week course, including jobseeking and interview skills, CV writing and a four-week work placement.

'We risk a potential backlash and misunderstanding over what positive discrimination is, but I firmly believe it is necessary to redress the present imbalance,' says Rahman.

Harassment at work

What is harassment?
Behaviour which is unwelcome or unacceptable and which results in the creation of a stressful or intimidating environment for the recipient.

What forms can harassment take?
– Verbal abuse
– Racist jokes
– Graffiti
– Embarrassing and/or insensitive comments
– Leering
– Physical contact
– Unwanted sexual advances
– Ridicule
– Isolation
– Victimisation

What should employers do?
Develop:
- A published, well-promoted policy statement with top management support
- Clear, fair and user-friendly procedures for resolving problems quickly and confidentially
- Counselling, advice and support mechanisms for recipients
- Thorough and immediate investigation methods for alleged incidents
- Swift, sensitive and effective remedies
- Appropriate grievance and disciplinary procedures
- A sustained programme of communication, monitoring and training.

© Department for Education and Employment

You don't have to be white to be a racist

By Steve Doughty, Social Affairs Correspondent

Whites are not the only people who show racial prejudice, a New Labour think-tank declared yesterday.

Blacks, Asians and Jews can be just as hostile in their attitudes to other groups, a survey found.

The inquiry for the Institute of Public Policy Research – the research group reputed to be closest to the thinking of Tony Blair – appears to explode the myth propagated by race relations experts that only white racism matters.

The Institute said prejudice among whites is fuelled by their fear that English identity no longer counts. Society should be careful to nurture the pride of the groups within it.

Findings are to be presented to political leaders later this year. The Institute's view may herald a split over how to treat race issues between New Labour and the hardliners of the race relations industry, particularly in Left-wing local councils.

The survey, carried out for the think-tank by NOP and Opinion Leader Research, asked questions of 933 whites, 252 Afro-Caribbeans, 282 Asians, and 252 Jews. It found that only six in 100 whites believe there is no racism in Britain, but that more people are worried about crime and unemployment than they are about race.

The most arresting findings, however, were those that showed the attitude of various groups to each other.

Pollsters asked whether members of groups would mind if a close relative were to marry someone from another group.

Results showed 24 per cent of whites would mind either a lot or a little if a relative married an Afro-Caribbean. But so would 46 per cent of Asians and 48 per cent of Jews.

If the relative were to marry an Asian, 28 per cent of whites would mind, 18 per cent of Afro-Caribbeans, and 47 per cent of Jews.

When the relative was said to have married a Jew, 15 per cent of whites said they would mind, 19 per cent of Afro-Caribbeans, and 40 per cent of Asians.

Figures were higher when people were asked if they thought others of their racial group would mind relatives marrying outside it. Nearly two-thirds of whites, 63 per cent, said they thought most whites would object to marriage of a relative to an Afro-Caribbean.

Some pollsters believed at first that the high figures were a result

Q. Would you personally mind or not if one of your close relatives were to marry a person of Afro-Caribbean origin?

	White	Asian	Jewish
Mind a lot	13	32	29
Mind a little	11	14	19
Don't mind	74	47	46
Don't know	2	6	6

Q. Would you personally mind or not mind if one of your close relatives were to marry a person of Asian origin?

	White	Afro-Car	Jewish
Mind a lot	13	10	27
Mind a little	15	8	20
Don't mind	70	71	46
Don't know	2	6	6

Q. Would you personally mind or not mind if one of your close relatives were to marry a person of the Jewish faith?

	White	Afro-Car	Asian
Mind a lot	5	10	30
Mind a little	10	9	10
Don't mind	83	65	42
Don't know	2	12	17

Q. Do you agree that most refugees arriving in Britain are in need of our help and support?

	White	Afro-Car	Asian	Jewish
Definitely agree	33	29	18	35
Tend to agree	42	46	43	44
Neither	7	9	16	8
Tend to disagree	10	8	14	7
Definitely disagree	6	–	4	6
Don't know	3	9	5	1

not of prejudice, but of strong religious belief among Asians and Jews. However, a series of focus groups underlined the wide racial mistrust.

One Sikh told his group Britain was becoming more racist. 'Even Moslem, Sikh, Hindu and West Indian are picking on each other,' he said.

Pollsters said their studies showed that English whites were fearful over their own cultural identity and worried that ethnic groups did not share their values.

This lay behind fears over loss of jobs and status, they said. The pollsters also looked at attitudes to refugees. They found three-quarters of white people thought asylum seekers were in need of help and support – and that the greatest hostility to refugees was among Asians.

Many people blamed television for creating racism. One man told a focus group: 'Television is where you get most of your opinions from.'

IPPR researcher Yasmin Alibhai-Brown said: 'We have to look at inter-ethnic prejudice to see what we can do about it.

'We would be doing a great disservice if we did not talk about this issue.'

Looking to the future

Have we become a more equal society in the last twenty years? As an important new campaign against racism gets under way, Hannah Pool looks at the status of Britain's ethnic minorities

The European Year Against Racism was launched last Thursday at the European Parliament's headquarters in The Hague. The aims of the initiative are to highlight the threat and problems caused by racism and xenophobia across Europe.

1997 is also the 20th anniversary of the setting up of the Commission for Racial Equality (CRE). While much has improved since 1977, when the CRE was established, the status of the ethnic minorities in the UK is still by no means equal to that of the white population. Chris Myant, of the CRE, explains: 'A lot has happened in the last 20 years. More than anything the successes we have notched up show it is unnecessary for discrimination to continue for the next 20 years. Key parts of British society have begun to respond well to the fact we are a multiracial community but the overall problems of inequality still remain.'

Although racism is less acceptable than it was several years ago, it still exists. For example, only last week the car manufacturer Ford paid seven Asian and Afro-Caribbean workers at its Dagenham plant more than £70,000 compensation for racial discrimination after

Home ownership

One of the biggest differences among ethnic groups is home ownership. According to the 1991 Census, those from the South Asian communities are most likely to own their homes, at 77 per cent. Over 66 per cent of the white population own their home, compared to only 42 per cent of the black community.
The figures showing the percentage of people living in local authority accommodation are in direct contrast to this. Thirty-seven per cent of the black community live in council-owned property, compared with 21 per cent and 11 per cent of the white and South Asian communities.

Owner-occupied houses by ethnic group in Great Britain, 1991

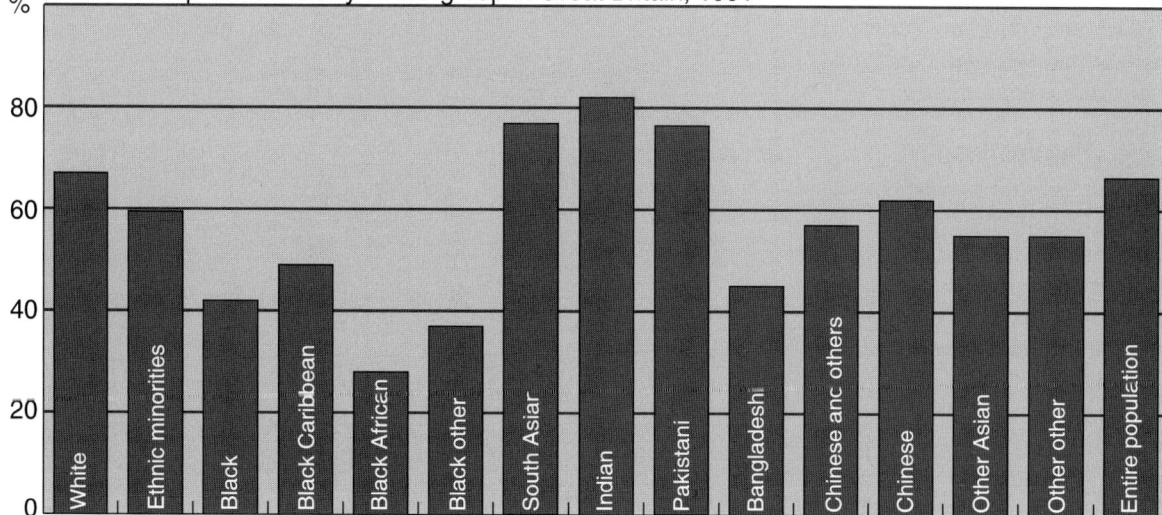

Source: 1991 Census Local Base Statistics

they were turned down for jobs in the company's élite driving fleet.

One example of the multi-cultural society we live in is the number of people involved in mixed-race relationships. The 1991 Census found that black men are the most likely of any ethnic group to be married to or living with people of different ethnic origin. Over 30 per cent of black men aged 16–24 and in a stable relationship are living with a white partner, compared with 23 per cent of black women and 1 per cent of white men and women. Although there are no earlier figures for comparison, it is widely believed this is an increasing trend.

But mixed-race couples are not acceptable to everybody. Only a few weeks ago a number of famous couples, in mixed-race relationships, were the subject of a letter-bombing campaign by a right-wing neo-Nazi group.

Initiatives such as the European Year Against Racism are positive ways of hammering home the message that such racial prejudice has no place in Europe in the '90s.

Ethnic minorities are doing better than their white counterparts in some areas – such as post-school education – and much worse in others – such as employment. There have been numerous advances in the fight against racism, but there are still too many sections of society in which people from ethnic minorities are not yet treated equally.

NB: For the purposes of this article, the terms black and white have been used when those involved have chosen to describe themselves as such.

Publications

CRE, *Roots of the Future: Ethnic Diversity in the making of Britain*, 1996.
Labour Force Survey, Summer 1995 – Spring 1996.
Mayhew *et al*: *The 1992 British Crime Survey*, Home Office research study 132, London, HMSO.
The New Nation newspaper, Gateway House, Milverton Street, London SE11 4AP. Tel 0171 793 8282.
© *The Guardian February, 1997*

Youth unemployment rates

Averages for June 1995 – May 1996 (% of economically active 16 to 24 year-olds)

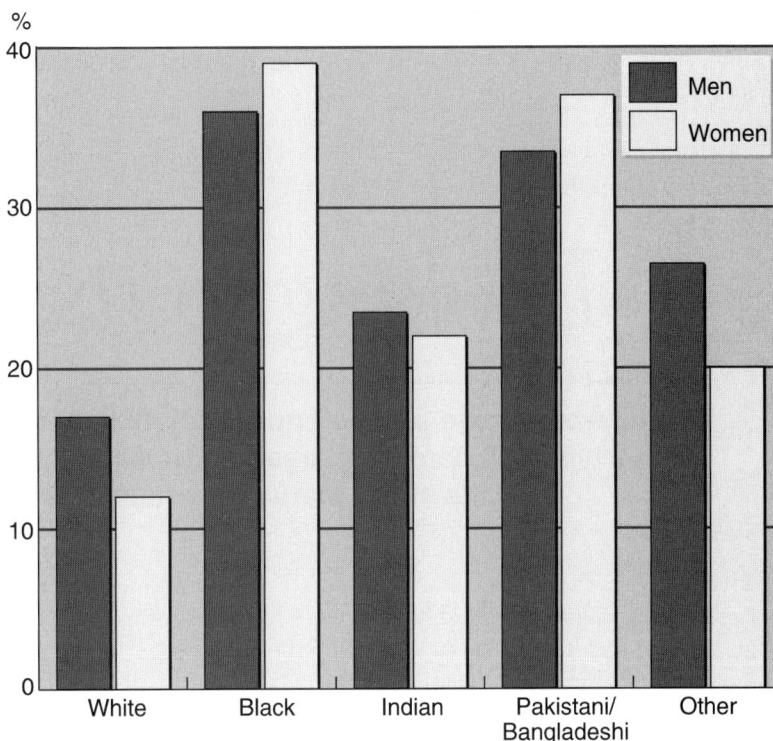

Source: Labour Force Survey

Ethnic populations in Britain

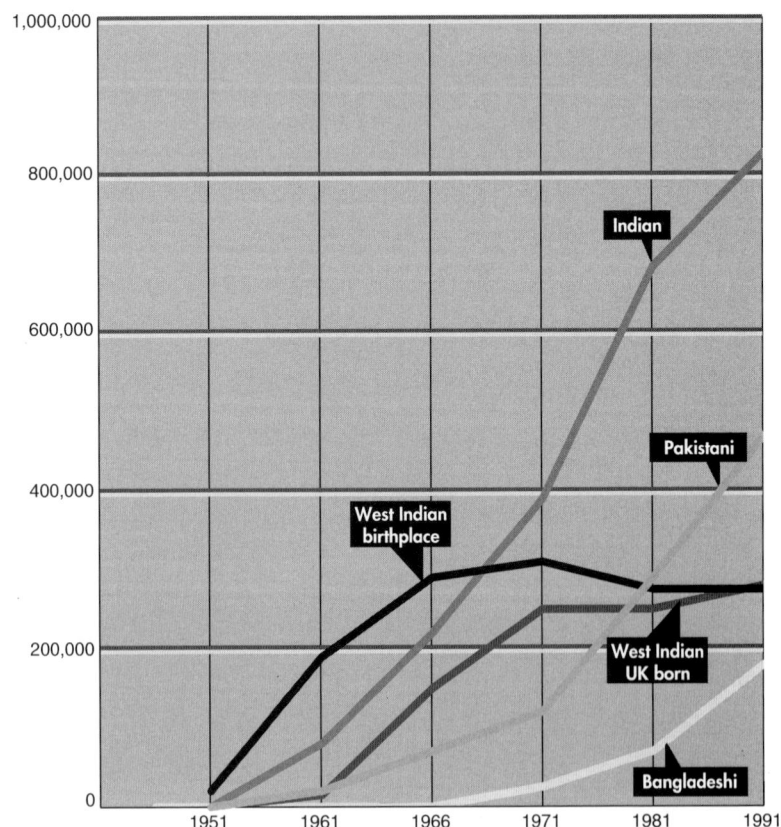

Source: Ethnicity in the 1991 Census, ONS, HMSO

Positive action

Promoting racial equality in employment

What is positive action?

Positive action describes a range of measures which can be taken under the Race Relations Act 1976 to help provide equality of opportunity in employment for people from particular racial groups.

Measures include training for particular work, and encouragement to apply for particular work.

Training can also be provided to meet the special needs of people from particular racial groups.

Positive action does not allow racial discrimination in recruiting, selecting or promoting. Positive action is about fair competition – not removing competition.

Under-representation

Most positive action measures are lawful only if people of the racial group intended to benefit are under-represented in the work in question. Exactly what counts as under-representation in law varies according to circumstances. Anyone planning positive action measures should check which criteria apply, and ensure that those criteria are satisfied.

Definition of a racial group

For the purposes of positive action, a racial group is any group defined by reference to colour, race, nationality or ethnic or national origins. A person can be a member of more than one racial group. References in this article to 'race', 'racial origins' etc. have this wide meaning.

What employers can do

Where certain criteria are met, employers can provide training limited to employees from particular racial groups, and can encourage job applications from members of such groups.

Employers may also provide training and encouragement for non-employees.

References to relevant sections of the Race Relations Act 1976 are given in brackets.

Training for particular work

- Employers can train people of a particular racial group for particular work in which they are under-represented.

Employers may consider providing training for some of their existing employees who are members of racial groups which are under-represented in particular work in the workplace.
(Section 38)
This could, for example, take the form of:

- a management skills development programme for potential managers;
- training in supervisory skills; or
- training for skilled and specialist jobs.

Employers may also support training for people who are not their employees but are from racial groups which are under-represented in particular work across Great Britain or some smaller area:
(Section 37)

- directly, by providing or funding training in particular skills, perhaps with other employers or training organisations; or
- indirectly, by providing work experience placements for trainees being trained by other organisations.

Special needs training

- Employers can provide training, education or other assistance to meet certain special needs of a particular racial group.
(Section 35)
The most common example of special needs education is tuition in English for people whose first language is not English.

Encouragement to apply for jobs

- Employers can encourage people of a particular racial group to apply for jobs in which their group is under-represented.
(Section 38)
Employers may do this by including encouraging messages in job advertisements. Care is needed with the wording, to make sure that people from other racial groups who read such advertisements will not think their applications would be unwelcome or would not be considered fairly. It is helpful to mention that selection for jobs will be on merit, or that applicants will be judged against objective criteria.

- Employers may also encourage employees from particular racial groups to apply for other jobs or promotion where those groups are under-represented.
(Section 38)
Employers may do this by including encouraging messages in any vacancy notices they circulate in the workplace.

Restricting training and encouragement to men or women

Employers may decide to provide training or encouragement for women only, or men only, from particular racial groups. If so, they will need to ensure that their proposals meet the positive action criteria set by both the Race Relations Act 1976 and the Sex Discrimination Act 1975.

- The above is an extract from *Positive Action*, produced by the Employment Department.

© *Employment Department January, 1997*

INDEX

African-Caribbean school pupils 10,
    13, 21
Asians
    and crime 23
    football players 27
    and housing 23, 27
    and racial attacks 21, 27
    school pupils 10, 14, 27

black people
    British 21
    and crime 23, 26-7
    and the criminal justice system 8,
        20
    and education 27
    and racial attacks 21
    and unemployment 20, 22, 27
    see also young people, black
bullying, and racial abuse in schools
    3-4, 8, 9, 11-12

Commission for Racial Equality
    (CRE) 3, 5, 8, 9, 10, 21
    on racial attacks and harassment
        18-19
    and the status of ethnic minorities
        35
crime
    and black people 23, 26-7
    racially motivated 8, 30
criminal justice system, and ethnic
    minorities 7-8, 20

discrimination 1, 24
    direct and indirect 20
    in employment 32

educational qualifications
    ethnic minorities 27
        and employment 22
    race and gender 14
    see also schools
employment
    ethnic minorities 27, 32-3
    harassment at work 33
    promoting racial equality in 37
    and racial discrimination 35-6
    see also unemployment
European Year Against Racism 35,
    36

families
    mixed-race 6-7, 9, 25-6, 36
    and racism in the home 9, 15
football racism 27-8

health, and ethnic minorities 25
health services, and racial
    harassment 31
homelessness 16, 20, 23
housing
    authorities, and racial harassment
    31

Irish children 12, 21

Jews
    attacks on 21
    attitudes to race 34

mixed-race families 6-7, 9, 25-6, 36

Neighbourhood Watch 31

police
    and racial incidents 5, 18, 19, 29,
        30, 31
    stopping and searching black
people 20
positive action 37
poverty, and racism 16
prejudice 1
prisoners, from ethnic minorities 8,
    20
public attitudes
    to racial discrimination 20
    to racist issues 1, 34-5

Race Relations Act (1976) 19, 20,
    21, 37
race relations in Britain 24
racial harassment 18-19
    bullying in schools 3-4, 8, 9, 11-12
    defining 18, 30
    impact of 30-1
    and the law 19
    street attacks 18-19
    see also violence
racism, defining 1
racists
    characteristics of 1-2
    and housing 23
    reasons for holding views 2
    and unemployment 22-3
refugees, public attitudes to 34, 35
relationships, inter-racial 15, 25-6,
    36
    public attitudes to 34
religious minorities, children in
    school from 12
rural areas, black people in 21

schools
    and anti-racist education 7, 10
    bullying and racial abuse in 3-4,
        8, 9, 11-12
    and children from religious
        minorities 12
    ethnically mixed 13
    and mixed-race children 7
    racial abuse in Scottish 8
    racism in 21
    and tackling racial harassment 31
    'white flight' from 14
Scotland
    ethnic unemployment and job
        discrimination 32-3
    racial abuse in schools 8
    racial harassment 33
suicide, and young people's
    experiences of racism 3, 4

training, and racial equality 37

unemployment
    and black people 20, 22, 27
    and ethnic minorities 25, 27
        in Scotland 32-3
        young people 1, 32, 36
    and racism 16, 22-3

victims of racism 19
    see also young people
violence see racial harassment

white people, and racial harassment
    19
women
    Asian, and racial attacks 21
    black, and crime 26
    race and educational
        qualifications 14
    white women and black men 25,
        36

young people 1-17
    black
        experiences of racism 1, 3
        from mixed-race families 3, 6-7
        and race relations 24
        racial violence by 19, 21
        unemployed 1, 32, 36
        victims of racism 2-5, 8-9
            in schools 3-4, 8, 9, 11-12
            and suicide 3, 4
YRE (Youth Against Racism in
    Europe) 16, 22-3

Anne Frank Educational Trust (AFETUK)
Garden Floor
43 Portland Place
London
W1N 3AG
Tel: 0181 950 6476
Fax: 0181 420 4520
To promote the message of education against discrimination in any form.

Campaign Against Racist Laws
15 Kenton Avenue
Southall
Middlesex
UB1 3QF
Tel: 0181 571 1437
Campaigns throughout the UK against the Immigration Act 1971, the Nationality Act 1981, the Primary Rule and the use of passport controls within the country. Produces publications.

Catholic Association for Racial Justice (CARJ)
St Vincent's Community Centre
Talma Road
London
SW2 1AS
Tel: 0171 274 0024
Enables black and white Catholics to affirm the positive role and contribution of black Catholics within the Church and to work together locally and nationally on issues of racial justice in Church and society. To order the booklet *Countering Racism* it is necessary to pay p&p which is £1.50 plus 20% postage and packing.

ChildLine
2nd Floor Royal Mail Building
Studd Street
London N1 0QW
Tel: 0171 239 1000 (admin)
Fax: 0171 239 1001
ChildLine is the free, national helpline for children and young people in trouble or danger. It provides confidential phone counselling service for any child with any problem 24 hours a day. Produces publications. Children or young people can phone or write free of charge about problems of any kind. ChildLine, Freepost 1111, London N1 0BR, Tel: Freephone 0800 1111.

Commission for Racial Equality (CRE)
Elliot House
10-12 Allington Street
London
SW1E 5EH
Tel: 0171 828 7022
Fax: 0171 931 0429
The Commission for Racial Equality is working for racial equality for a just society, which gives everyone an equal chance to work, learn and live free from discrimination and prejudice, and from a fear of racial harassment and violence. The Commission produces a wide range of factsheets, reports, books and other resources. Ask for their publications list.

Churches Commission on Racial Justice
Council of Churches for Britain and Ireland
Interchurch House
35 – 41 Lower Marsh
London
SE1 7RC
Tel: 0171 620 4444
Fax: 0171 928 0010
The Commission was formed to monitor trends in race relations in British society.

Runnymede Trust
11 Princelet Street
London
E1A 6QH
Tel: 0171 600 9666
Fax: 0171 600 8529
Aims to eliminate all aspects of racism and discrimination. The trust produces a monthly bulletin, *The Runnymede Bulletin*, books and reports on racism.

The Football Association
Medical Education Centre
Lilleshall Hall National Sports Centre
Near Newport
Shropshire
TF10 9AT
Tel: 01952 605928
Fax: 01952 825 496
Provides information on racism in football.

The Tower Hamlets LDC
English Street
London
E3 4TA
Tel: 0181 983 1944
Fax: 0181 983 1932
Has published *Challenging Racism – The Activities Book*.

Youth against Racism in Europe (YRE)
PO Box 858
London
E9 5HU
Tel: 0181 533 4533
Youth against Racism in Europe is an international campaign involving young people against racism, fascism and forms of prejudice and discrimination. YRE has published a booklet called *Anti-racist Education*. The book is written by young people for young people and costs £5:00 (£2:50 for students and bulk orders of 10 or more copies.) Please add 50p for postage per copy. Cheques payable to YRE.

ACKNOWLEDGEMENTS

The publisher is grateful for permission to reproduce the following material.

While every care has been taken to trace and acknowledge copyright, the publisher tenders its apology for any accidental infringement or where copyright has proved untraceable. The publisher would be pleased to come to a suitable arrangement in any such case with the rightful owner.

Chapter One: Young people and racism

Stop racism now, © MIZZ, July 1996, *Victims of racism speak out*, © MIZZ, July 1996, *Despair of children in race jibes*, © Daily Express, July 1996, *Suicide agony of boy tormented by racists*, © Daily Express, October 1996, *Racism 'makes young try to rub off colour'*, © The Telegraph Plc, London 1996, *Racism incidents*, © Police Records, *Shades of prejudice*, © The Scotsman, *Call to guide children from evil of racism*, © Western Mail, August 1996, *Racial abuse is problem in Scots schools*, © The Herald, July 1996, *Ethnic minority children 'still suffer racism daily'*, © The Guardian, July 1996, *Ministers in school anti-racist drive*, © The Guardian, September 1996, *GCSEs*, © OFSTED, *Children and racism*, © ChildLine, *Where ethnic mix proves no barrier to success*, © The Guardian, September 1996, *Plight of a school shunned by whites*, © The Daily Mail, October 1996, *Education*, © IES, *'My racist parents hate my boyfriend'*, © Just Seventeen, September 1996, *Youth against Racism in Europe*, © Youth against Racism in Europe (YRE), 1996, *Beat it!*, © MIZZ, July 1996.

Chapter Two: Racism in the community

Racial attacks and harassment, © Commission for Racial Equality, 1995, *Racial incidents*, © Police Records, *Facts about racism in Britain*, © Cities in Schools – Tower Hamlets, 1995, *What the racists say*, © Youth against Racism in Europe (YRE), *Ethnic populations in Britain*, © HMSO, *CRE admits Britain has good record on race*, © The Guardian, June 1996, *Black and white facts of modern romance*, © The Daily Mail, August 1996, *Football racism*, © Kick it Out, *More race attacks reported to police*, © The Guardian, April 1996, *Violence round the country*, © HMSO reproduced with kind permission of Her Majesty's Stationery Office, *Tackling racial harassment*, © Crime Concern / Commission for Racial Equality, *Double whammy for minorities struggling to find work*, © Scotsman, October 1996, *Unemployment rates*, © HMSO reproduced with kind permission of Her Majesty's Stationery Office, *Harassment at work*, © Department for Education and Employment – HMSO reproduced with kind permission of Her Majesty's Stationery Office, *You don't have to be white to be a racist*, © The Daily Mail, February 1997, *Looking to the future*, © The Guardian, February 1997 *Home ownership*, © HMSO reproduced with kind permission of Her Majesty's Stationery Office, *Youth unemployment rates*, HMSO reproduced with kind permission of Her Majesty's Stationery Office, *Positive action*, © Employment Department – HMSO reproduced with kind permission of Her Majesty's Stationery Office.

Photographs and Illustrations

Pages 1, 13, 16, 24, 31, 33: Ken Pyne, pages 9, 11, 17, 25: Andrew Smith / Folio Collective, page 15: Katherine / Folio Collective.

Craig Donnellan
Cambridge
January, 1997